# The People's Histor

# Around Jarr

by

## John Carlson & Joyce Carlson

Girls' Training Corps officers pictured during the Second World War. Left to right: Ella Carr, Dorothy Hall (commander), unknown and Hilda Pattie. Both Dorothy Hall and Hilda Pattie also served as Headmistresses in the town.

*Previous page*: National Coal Board Sentinel Diesel locomotive number 104 hauls coal wagons specially converted for passenger use on an enthusiasts tour of the Bowes Railway in 1976. The location is the former level crossing near Monkton Village.

Copyright © John Carlson & Joyce Carlson 2000

First published in 2000 by

The People's History Ltd
Suite 1
Byron House
Seaham Grange Business Park
Seaham
Co. Durham
SR7 0PY

ISBN 1 902527 45 3

# Contents

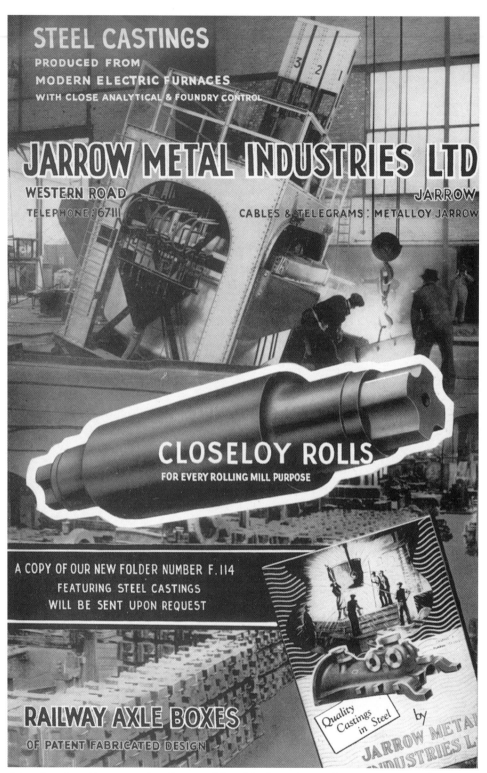

A trade advertisement for Jarrow Metal Industries Ltd, Western Road.

# Introduction

This book is a collection of pictorial and verbal snapshots of the town of Jarrow and its surrounding area. The content has been gathered largely by asking people we know, or their friends, if they have or know anything interesting about Jarrow. This is not an attempt to write a history of the town, or even place the material included here in an absolute context. Like the geologist making test bores through strata we don't know what's really down there, we just know what we have brought up.

While the town's legal borders may have changed over time it's also true that what the individual instinctively feels is Jarrow, and what is not, varies according to their family history, where they have worked and where they have spent their leisure time. Therefore, this book's scope is as flexible as its cover, and although we have generally stayed clear of South Shields and drawn the line at Brockley Whins Station, we have included the Bede Trading Estate, some of Simonside and Hebburn.

The photographic content is drawn from a number of sources and the photographers who made the original images would have done so with a variety of intents. Many are from picture postcards. Some are views that would be taken from carefully optimised perspectives and bought by people familiar either with the whole town, or just a hotel, or a street, where they had stayed while visiting friends, relations or on business. Other cards may have been

The delivery drivers of Jarrow and Hebburn Co-operative Society at the Salem Street Garage. Included are: Jim Preston, Jimmy McKlusky, John Monks and Bob Turnbull.

*A locomotive driver's view of the Jarrow Station curve from one of the world's most famous engines, the A3 Pacific 4472 'Flying Scotsman', in 1968.*

given free to the sender, having been printed with the sole object of advertising a place, or a product, or a particular point of view.

Also included are 'official' photographs, formal in every way. Group and individual portraits of men and women and clinical images of machines that represent past, or only the beginnings of, years filled with negotiation, development, frustration and compromise. When taken, the contents would reflect an individual's position, their power relative to each other, and the overall standing of the group. In many cases the complex story behind these photographs has now been lost or fractured and they are offered here with what information we could assemble.

Also here are 'amateur' photographs, family or individual snapshots often taken in an unplanned moment and are a chance recording of lives that would otherwise be little covered by official photographs. Sometimes they represent the typical, sometime the untypical and show something of the diversity of life in Jarrow.

Much of the text in this book is drawn directly from the memories of Jarrow residents, recorded on cassette tape during 1999, and then transcribed almost directly on to the printed page. Also present are reports drawn from the long defunct local papers the *Jarrow Guardian* and the *Jarrow Express*. One or two of the events and controversies that have shaped the town have been touched upon.

# A CHILD'S EYE VIEW

*Carnivals And Bands … Going To School … Games To Play …*
*Through The War … New Horizons … Thinking About Work …*

Two thousand local children visiting Palmer's Shipbuilding and Iron Company yard in Jarrow, *circa* 1904. Rather than being there on a school outing, their presence may have been required to aid the welcome of a group of potential shipbuyers. Such visits would have been of great importance to the town. In spite of a recent financial crisis many of the children would then have seen the yard as their future, providing work for the men and in turn housekeeping money for the women. However, by the time many of the boys here would be out of apprenticeship the First World War would be claiming many young men's lives and many of their girlfriend's futures. While some of those working 'at home' in Palmer's yard would find themselves under attack from what had only years before been seen as one of the miracles of the scientific age, the airship.

A Jarrow street carnival, *circa* 1920. Long time Jarrow resident, Con Shiels, actively participated in many carnivals and parades. He recalls: 'I joined the Jarrow Burnside Band and when we were on parade we used to be dressed up as sheikhs. Talk about impressive! We had a little mirror on the front of our turbans and when the sun shone on those the people in the crowd were blinded. It was marvellous.

We used to travel around the North which was great for the likes of me because we were going as far as Ashington and Consett and Barnard Castle even. Our vision could easily have been bounded by Jarrow. Many people never went further than South Shields. You knew every street, every field, every farmer within six miles of Jarrow. You knew that lot because that was all there was.'

A decorated horse-drawn laundry van owned by Jarrow and Hebburn Co-operative Society in Wilberforce Street. It had apparently just won first prize in the horse and harness section.

Jarrow residents John and Diana Daniels in 1920. The costumes would be
similar to many worn in local carnivals.

A contemporary carnival was described in the local press.

Under a grey sky, Jarrow made merry on Saturday, a monster procession over a
mile and a half in length transversing the streets to raise money for the
Mayor's Emergency Distress Fund. The procession was headed by the King and
Queen of Carnival who were followed by over 20 jazz bands, the performers
gaily attired in carnival costumes, and by an army of Clowns, Jesters, Dixie
Minstrels, Redskins, Bandits, and other grotesque characters. There was a good
turn out of decorated horses and vehicles, and among the many amusing
features of the procession was a mock circus, with some exceptionally lively
performers. The finals of the jazz band contests were held on Charlton's Field
where a fair kept the fun going far into the night. Prizes were presented by the
Mayoress, the principal awards being as follows – Best tableau: Maypole; Best
trade advertisement: Henderson's of Gateshead; Ladies' fancy costume: Alice
Glease (Indian Squaw); Comic costume: Mrs Bell; Individual novelty:
E. Brown; Best decorated ladies' cycle: Irene Lambert; Best male impersonator:
Jennie Glease (toreador); Best individual novelty (schoolgirl): A. Nesworthy
(fishwife); Largest muster: Dixie Minstrels, South Shields; Club causing most
fun: Jarrow R.O.A.B; Individual causing most fun: John Grey, South Shields;
Best groomed horse, heavy class: C. Sayers, Willington Quay; Light class:
T. Robinson, Jarrow; Best decorated horse: Jarrow Corporation; Best fancy
costume: H. Lake, Cullercoats; Best decorated cycle: D. Storer; Best lady
impersonator: J. Mason; Best individual novelty (schoolboy): T.W. Serle,
South Shields.

Cyril Daniels with his sister Irene in Jarrow West Park, 1929. Cyril has long been active in politics in the town.

Class 5A of St Bede's School, Jarrow. Con Shiels is fourth from right, first row. He remembers: 'Even though the classes were packed I think we had a good education. Unfortunately we could only get so far. I passed this particular exam to get into St Cuthbert's Grammar School. It broke my dad's heart. He told me he couldn't even afford to pay my fare to get there and my education stopped dead. Who knows what may have happened to me. Who knows!'

Stan Tweddell and his brother George. They also had a sister, Jenny, not pictured. While Stan spent much of his own working life in the painting and decorating industry, his immediate family have been associated with the pub trade. Stan recalls: 'I was born in the old Prince of Wales Hotel in the room under the sign. My dad, Billy Tweddell, sometimes called Ginger Billy, worked for Newcastle Breweries as a pub manager. It was a very strict firm to work for. I suppose we were fairly well off with him being in the pub trade. You had your trouble, but managers could always handle it. If an argument started the manager would tell them 'out' and out they went. The manager was the boss as far as who got through the door and the brewers never bothered them over that.

Commercial Road was a very close area then, close together houses and everyone knowing everyone else. Then before the Second World War the council started shipping people up to the new estates around Primrose, the area started to get a little bit lonely, and they started to pull the houses down.

Then we all moved over to a pub called the Staith House. That had a roaring trade from the Mercantile Dry Dock. People coming off the ferry were calling in and I think a lot of people preferred the Newcastle Breweries beer to what they served at The Commercial. If the publican kept his nose clean he could have a bit entertainment on and the police never bothered him. They would allow an accordion or a banjo as long as there was no trouble. With being so near the river the water rats used to come up into the cellar and my dad used to have to catch them. Even though he worked in the pub business he was a riveter by trade. When the war started he went down to sign on for the army, but he was told that a riveter was a reserved occupation and even if the army let him in he would just be called back to the yards. He managed to work in the shipyards by day while he had someone looking after the pub, then he was back behind the bar again at night.

Upstairs we had a long front room. If anyone owned a three piece suite, then the room it was put in you would call a front room. From our front room my brother George and I could see right over the gas yard, right out into the Tyne. During the war we saw most of the ships coming in and out, I think we knew every ship, even down to the dredgers. My brother had a book where he would keep a record of their movements. We saw the *Kelly* coming in when it was practically under water. If we read in the paper that a ship was sunk we would mark them off, sunk by U-boat, by mine, whatever. Men from ships that had been involved in conflict would come in our pub while their ship was in dock, some of them would be our best customers while repairs were underway. You could often tell without being told that work was near completion and their ship was getting ready to sail. Then through our upstairs window my brother and I would watch their ships sail out, then we would read in the paper, sunk with all hands. It was a sad time.

At the Prince of Wales we had a stable, most pubs had one. There was a fella who worked from there called Jack Russell. He delivered lemonade for a local lemonade company. He would go over on the ferry to North Shields and Wallsend, he was always out on his rounds. When the school holidays came my mother used to give me and my brother some sandwiches and we would go off with him on his horse and cart all over the north side of the river. It was a great day out for us. When he retired the stable was rented out to Archie Foster the coal man. He was there for years until he handed the business over to his son. Then the coal men started to use wagons and that was the end of the horse and carts.'

A horse drawn delivery wagon belonging to R. Andison, Wine and Spirit Merchants. The location of this photograph is unknown although the firm was based in North Street and is thought to have ceased trading in 1956.

Stan Tweddell continues: 'On the other side of the Prince of Wales they had what we called a function room where the pigeon fanciers used to hold social evenings. Then we had the voting taking place next door in St Peter's Hall. We used to vote for the Mayor in those days.

Sometimes in the pub we used to have Carling days. My mother used to put the Carlings on in a big boiler. They were like big grey peas. You could even buy them at the shops in a big paper cone to eat in the street. We used to have broth, stottie cake, sandwiches, the men used to get up and do their turns, tap dance, play the banjo, accordion – it was a real good time. The kids used to run about the floor till about eight o'clock and then just fall asleep.

We had a game called Bomb Baters. We had sheets of paper wrapped up and tied up with string and we whacked each other with it and called out 'Bomb Bater'. We used to ask each other, 'green peas or barley?' If you were a Protestant and they said, 'green peas', that meant they were a Catholic, so you whacked them! Or if you said, 'barley', a Catholic would whack you. It never got aggressive. It was just something you used to do.

A crowd of us would find four or five old car or wagon tyres and we would bool them about all night. If someone was really little they would get themselves inside a wagon tyre and we would bool them down the bank.

At T. Fraser, the decorators in Ormonde Street, the painters' barrows used to stand outside the back shop. If you were a kid and the barrows were there it was a done thing to get the barrows, run along with them, with the wheels clanking over the road, and let them go into the barriers at the bottom with the apprentices chasing after you. Strangely enough I went on to work at Fraser's.

The Golden Fleece in Commercial Road near to Jarrow pit heap. Marks left by the removal of the tramlines are visible on the road.

13

If we wanted to see a film we had the Regal, the Picture House and the Empire. My dad was always on his day off and he used to take us to first house pictures. At the Regal Cinema on a Saturday morning it was a penny to get in and you got a bar of chocolate.

I went to St Peter's School. It was a small Church of England School on the land that Rohm and Hass has now, down by where the ferry was. All of our family went to that school. There was a church attached to the building and we had our own vicar called Vicar Williams. The war interfered with our schooling. We couldn't go to school for a while because they hadn't enough shelters, so a lot of us were sent to Jarrow Hall. My brother used to go in the morning, I went in the afternoon and then it would change round. Other children were in people's front rooms in Croft Terrace and Bede Burn Road. I think we were down to three hours a day for four days a week at one point. We always had our gas masks with us. Once a barrage balloon, stationed a few hundred yards up the road, got away and wrapped itself around the church steeple and just pulled it off. The whole Tyne was thick with balloons at the time, even the ships could carry them.

A lot of the teachers were called up, almost all of the young men went and they had to bring a lot of teachers out of retirement. Some of the schools used to hold boxing. We got a new teacher called Mr Campbell and if it was ever raining when it was PT time he would shift the desks in the classroom and say, "Right that's going to be the ring." Then he gave us a big box of boxing gloves and told us to find a pair that fit. Then it was, "You and you! You and you! Get in the ring!" Very few used to refuse. Often it was best of pals knocking the daylights out of each other.'

The Royal, Market Square – known as the Theatre Bar. The theatre entrance is on the left. Just visible, to the extreme left, is the Co-op Cafe and Cake Shop.

Olive Goldsbrough (*right*) in her parents' back garden at Monkton Village. Olive recalls: 'I was born in Jarrow but when I was about a year old we moved to Elmfield Road near Monkton Village. Cars were a rarity but there were hay carts and farm tractors moving about all the time. At night it was very dark walking the village, past the Lord Nelson pub and up this little cart track. It wasn't a proper road. We used to call it, 'the sleepers', because it was made either from old wooden railway sleepers or pit props. I lived at, 'The Sinkers Cottages'. There were about twenty of them. I believe they were built for the people who were to sink the colliery at Monkton, but when I lived there they were often used by workers from the cokeworks. Inside were all the mod cons of the time – ours had hot water from a big range in the kitchen. They were quite modern compared to what was available in 1937.

During the war there were barrage balloons moored on the golf course, huge things with stabilisers on. They looked like enormous elephants with ears. One got loose and floated towards the houses and a kid from next door came running into our back room in fear. We were bombed a few times. I think they were trying to hit the cokeworks. Near our houses was a great big gun, and when it went off you could hear it and feel the vibration.

It was a while until we got our own air raid shelter and we used to have to share with the people of a house five doors down. Our own turned out to be very small. It looked like a mound with a little door. The shelters were always getting waterlogged, but they were marvellous after the war because of the frogs! They were full of frogs. I suppose they were death traps really.

On the evenings I could go to the pictures in Jarrow if I wanted to but there was always the matter of getting home to Monkton Village. The buses didn't run that late and if you were accompanied on the journey back by a boyfriend you always had to allow for a bus for him to get back home as well. In Monkton Village itself there wasn't that much social life. It certainly wasn't the done thing for women to go into pubs, not that there were very many of them about anyway.

Monkton Stadium was just a little running track. I think it was paid for by the metal industry and the tubeworks. My brother used to work in the tubeworks and I used to go there for the sports days and I remember winning prizes. There was a football pitch in the middle for Jarrow Football Team and a cinder track around the edges for running on. But now it's all posh!'

Monkton Village, 'then and then'. Little appears to have changed between the above views although of course housing would be springing up in the surrounding fields and new and/or better roads would be changing people's 'mental maps' of the district. The above image is from the Robinson's Real Photo Series, while the one below is part of the Connacher Collection. It's not known if the second was deliberately posed to provide a contrast with the first.

Michael and Maureen Nellist aged three months: Michael recalls: 'On a Sunday night me and my mates would play on a large piece of spare ground at the bottom of the street that went down to the river. We used to hunt for crabs under the rocks, go fishing in the Tyne and play with knives and bows and arrows. We had bonfires down there and we also made camps under the ground. With my father, John, we would visit Uncle Joe and Aunt Dolly our relations in Palmer Street. We would also visit Jessie's Fish and Chip shop in Frobisher Street, Hebburn.

'My father worked at the local iron foundry that we called, 'the metals,' the Armstrong Whitworth factory then called the Davy Roll Co Ltd. He and my mother Elizabeth had married in 1936 at St Bede's Catholic Church. By the time my twin sister and I came a long in 1948 we lived just two streets away from 'the metals' at number 27 Franklin Street in an old two bedroomed ground floor flat. Two adults and four children, I have an elder brother John and a sister Betty, we all lived together in that small flat. I always remember the dust that came from the metals and covered everything including the washing stretched out on the clothes line. Inside there was often the smell of bread and cakes baking in the black fire range in the living room. I left school at fifteen and started work the following week in the Jarrow and Hebburn Co-operative Society Store. I was on the mobile shops and my first boss was Sammy Purvis who went on to become the steward of the Alberta Club. On my first day I reported to the Co-op garage in Salem Street and was told to wait in the cab of the mobile bus shop. I waited and waited and gradually the excitement of starting work turned to boredom and I began to explore the cab. All of a sudden the bus began to roll backwards and then someone jumped into the cab and just as suddenly the van slammed to a stop. I must have knocked the hand break off, but luckily the van was stopped before it did any damage although I felt this was not the best start to my first day at work. After a while on the mobile shops I worked in various branches of the Co-op, Birch Street, Wansbeck Road and Lion Street. Then I moved to Cigarette Components on the Bede Estate and then in 1975 I started working for myself in the aquatic business and have been doing that ever since.'

Michael and Maureen Nellist dressed for their First Communion, *circa* 1955.

John, Elizabeth, Michael and Maureen Nellist, Christmas, 1952.

Michael and Maureen Nellist with their mother and friends, Angus Bradley and John Douglas, beside the River Tyne, *circa* 1958.

*Above*: Members of Christ Church Girls' Brigade, 1928. *Below*: Children of Grange School, standard 1, the date is likely to be the mid 1940s.

*Right*: Children from Ellison Church of England School, February 1940. They were about to be evacuated to St John's Church School in Shildon. Included are:
J. Sayers, J. Urwin W. Sayers,
F. Harrison,
G. Whitup,
J. Wilson, Isabel Stapylton and Alma Charlton.

The pictures on this and the facing page are of Bilton Hall County Infants School at the time of its opening. Bilton Hall was the first school in Jarrow to be planned and built after the Second World War and was formally opened by County Councillor W. Brown on Tuesday 6th November 1951. The first Headmistress was Marjorie Hall. Although the 1950s are often seen as the dawn of a new age for social provision and planning, many of these ideas had been political currency well before the war. The school was built to cater for around 120 children of the ages of 5-7, many of whom already lived close to the school but previously had to travel to one of the older schools in the centre of the town. Each classroom had fitted windows intended to allow in the maximum amount of sunlight and fresh air and had its own running water supply. Each child was also given their own locker. The school hall was intended for all kinds of physical and artistic activity as well as being the school dining room with an adjoining kitchen.

Con Shiels with a number of other young men from the area working in London in the 1930s.

Neil Tweddell, left, with Julian Varley in Neil's parents' back garden in Glasgow Road, *circa* 1982. While the youth of the 1980s never had it so bad as many of the children of the pre-war days, the recessions of the 1980s drastically cut the employment opportunities open to those just coming on to the labour market who found apprenticeships and traditional employment opportunities had virtually disappeared. For many life after

school suddenly became one long enforced holiday paid for by the DHSS. Although able to appreciate some of the opportunities of life denied to their parents who were almost propelled into work the day after leaving school, many later found they had no choice but to move out of the area if they were ever to work. In his case Neil moved to London and a managerial career with several high profile clothing companies.

# A WORKING
# ENVIRONMENT

*Industrial Hazards … Palmer's Yard … Conditions Of Work …*
*Carrying Coals … Steel And Metals … Delivery Drivers …*

A locomotive blasts through Jarrow goods yard with a train of oil wagons. The date is likely to be September 1966. In many ways this photograph can be said to illustrate some of the tensions in the town. The power and the needs of industry (and the need for industry itself) against the desire for peaceful living environments. The battle between the old and the new Jarrow. The new fighting to emerge from the decay of the old or the old and trusted features struggling to survive against the clinical and characterless new – either or both, depending on your point(s) of view. It's noticeable that while many of the buildings in the foreground have gone those beyond the railway have largely survived.

# Jarrow Colliery

Sunk by Simon Temple, Jarrow Colliery's opening in September 1803 is often regarded as the beginning of industry in the town. The colliery was virtually shut by 1851 the year before Palmer launched the *John Bowes*, although an 1856 map shows the colliery and a wagonway to a riverside staith still in place, although by now surrounded by railways, a pottery, chemical works and ballast hills. The industry of that time was hardly environmentally friendly. Waste was often dumped wherever the producer could get away with it and abandoned plant left to decay leaving a legacy of dereliction.

This laissez faire attitude and the difficulties authorities had in dealing with it can be glimpsed in the *Jarrow Guardian's* coverage of an 1887 inquest. Six children had died when part of a road from under which they were gathering coals collapsed on top of them. Extracts are reproduced below:

George Stockman, a painter at a Jarrow shipyard, and living at 22, Pearson Place, said: 'Sarah Elizabeth Stockman was my daughter, and was fourteen years and nine months old. I came home from work on Friday afternoon a little after five o'clock and while I was washing my hands before taking tea, Mrs Mahoney, a neighbour cried out, "For God's sake, Mr Stockman go and save my child!" I ran to the spot and saw three heads, the other parts of the bodies being covered with the 'debris'. Some men were digging when I got there to get the children out. The first I saw taken out was the dead body of a boy, and it was taken to Geddes' public house. Others were exposed and the earth was taken away. Margaret Mahoney's dead body was then taken out, and I assisted to take it home. When I got home I said where's my Bessie? And the mother said, "She'll be here just now," but I was not satisfied, and when I went back I found that I had been standing near her body before. I afterwards carried her body home. My children do not generally gather coals, but since that place has been opened they have gone. I have five other children, and will be more careful in future that they did not go to such places.'

Patrick King ten years of age said he resided at Milton Street and had attended school since he was six years old, and still went; cannot read much. Went to the place to gather coals after he came from school. About 1.30 he got his dinner, and then some girls came for him to go for coals and he went over to where the 'big hole' is near the chemical factory. Other boys and girls were there when he went digging for coals under the roadway. All were working together with the exception of a few in the hole. When the roadway fell he was right under the road which hung over him. He was hurt, but not much as he was the second brought out and was taken away at once.

By the Coroner: 'His father was a labourer at Palmer's ship yard, but did not work constant. He had five children. None of the others went for coal because they were too young. When he went he took a blanket, an apron and a small poker.'

Witness: 'Nobody complained to me of the road being dangerous. The upper crust, which is heavy, and which has crushed the children so much, is formed of burnt pyrites.'

The Coroner: 'Mr Russell here said that thirty years ago the original road ran parallel to the ballast hills. Coal refuse was at the bottom of the present road which was covered with chemical 'scars'. Attempts had been made to stop the road up, but that could not be done.'

The Coroner in summing up said that it might be a public footpath, but it was not a public road. If it was a public foot path and they even found the responsible parties, he did not think that the court had anything to do with that, because the children had no business to be there, and were trespassers; consequently by their and somebody else's unlawful act the accident had been caused. For what had happened the children were directly at fault and their parents indirectly; and further, the parents who had sent the children out for coals were censurable in the highest degree.

The Coroner, continuing, said large numbers of children and grown up persons were engaged in this dangerous occupation throughout the district, whether on railway lines and on heaps; and it could not be too well known that it was not only wrong but dangerous, and in the present case no-one was to blame but the children and their parents. It was unfortunate that the accident should have happened but the only difference between this case and others was that there had been six deaths instead of one, the facts otherwise being similar. The children could have had no better warning than that given by the witness McLauglin, but they ignored him and took no notice. He could only suggest that a verdict of accidental death be returned.

Mr T. Todd, a juror, quite agreed with the verdict but he thought it was a case that should not be allowed to pass over without being taken as a precedent for extra supervision being exercised over the district, and for the prevention of accidents of a similar character. He was not aware what officer of the Borough the work fell to but someone should see that the children, who had little idea of the danger incurred, were prevented from going to such places. There might be other places in the Borough that would be well to look to.

A verdict of 'Accidental Death' was returned.

Palmer's Jarrow yard, seen across Blackett Street/Western Road *circa* 1920. By this time the sheer scale of the enterprise would have been difficult to capture in a single image, although in the authors' opinion this photograph comes close. This is the iron and steelworks, the famous cranes can be glimpsed in the background. The two steel structures running across the picture are actually the supports for a travelling crane. We suspect the picture was taken from the roof of the former ordinance works. Today Newcastle-bound Metro travellers can make a 'then and now' comparison by turning their heads sharply to the right as their train sweeps over the old Bowes Railway bridge and looking towards the Rohm and Haas factory. The view has certainly changed.

Palmer was a coalowner who saw the advantages of industrial integration. He became involved in building engine powered iron colliers because to stay competitive with southern pits he needed to move his coal to London at lower costs than wooden powered sails ships could manage. This he spectacularly did in 1852 with the first screw collier, the *John Bowes*. Palmer later commented that when the ability of the *John Bowes* to cut the cost of carrying coals to London became apparent he faced the combined hostility of established shipowners, builders, crew and many of the associated industries. Tugs even tried to run the *John Bowes* aground. In the next two years alone Palmer's built 25 similar vessels and increasingly the advantages of smelting and rolling his own steel right next to his own shipbuilding yard became apparent.

One of the ships that Palmer's built in 1905, the navy cruiser HMS *Sapphire*.

While Jarrow has never been a one-industry town, it has never had another industry like Palmer's and more than sixty years after its cranes were toppled by the demolition men it's arguable that the dust has not yet entirely settled for the people of the town. Several books chronicle the yard's rise and decline and debate whether Palmer's role was as an exploiter of the town and its workforce, or as a benefactor, at least of sorts. Most contemporary writings on Palmer now seem almost craven in tone. Then to many people men like Palmer, who seemed to create wealth out of thin air, were possessors of near god-like powers. And while Ellen Wilkinson's book *The Town That Was Murdered* contains much useful information the overall tone is perhaps a little too accusatory. While the works did bring squalor as well as wages its difficult to decide if Palmer felt the social problems his works were creating were any of his responsibility or if his documented attempts to alleviate problems such as poor housing were done out of altruism or self-interest.

The engines of the *Sapphire*.

Palmer's blast furnaces. This view is possibly from the riverside. The picture comes from a guide dated 1909 but it is possibly earlier. Although the yard is long gone several guidebooks, journals and catalogues of its activities survive and through these we can glimpse some of its complex workings. This is from a Great Exhibition brochure:

'There are five blast furnaces of modern design, with the usual equipment of hot blast stoves. As a general rule these furnaces are worked three at a time. Each furnace being blown from a separate main, which can be alternatively coupled to any of the four blowing engines. The furnaces are all about 80 feet high, with hearths varying from 11 feet 6 inches to 13 feet in diameter, and are so arranged that the product can either be delivered in a molten state to the steelworks for the manufacture of steel, or cast into 'pigs' for delivery to the engineworks and foundries of the company, or as is the case with a large proportion of the output, delivered to customers over the whole of this country and abroad. The iron cast as pigs (pig iron) is lifted from the beds in combs by overhead electric cranes and delivered to an electrically driven machine which automatically breaks up and loads the pig iron into trucks, each pig bearing a distinguished brand, 'Jarrow' for the Cleveland quality and 'Tyneside' for the Hermatite. The blast furnaces are in direct connection with various railway systems and closely adjacent to the company's own deep-water wharf on the river at which steamers bringing the ore from Spain and North Africa, or alternatively smaller vessels bringing ore from the company's own mines in this country, are berthed, and this position permits all of the necessary raw materials, the several classes of production and the waste products being handled with a minimum of cost and effort.'

The landmark Palmer's cranes. Their operation was described in an industrial guide:

'A prominent feature in the yard is the instillation of overhead lifting and transportation trolleys consisting of cableways over the building berths, mounted on two inclined pivoted supports. On each cableway there is a trolley carriage from which the hoisting, lowering and cross transversal movements are controlled by one man. The approximate speed of longitudinal travel is 600 feet per minute. It will be seen that this system covers every part of the structure of the vessel being built each piece being lifted from the railway at the fore end of the berth and deposited in the proper position.'

Palmer's West Jetty and Sheerings.

The boiler shops south end (*above*) and (*below*) its north end. These images are from a guide dated 1909 although its likely they were taken some time before that. At that time they contained three large bays about 400 feet long and several smaller shops.

*Above*: Looking more like the engines of some futuristic space ship water-tube boilers in the boiler shop. *Below*: The exterior of the joiners' and cabinet-makers' shops.

*Above*: Ordinary marine boilers in the boiler shop. *Below*: The fitting shop. A 1920s guide to the yard stated: 'The engine shops at Jarrow comprises a light machine shop containing a full equipment of the smaller sizes of lathes, milling machines and other tools; a medium machine shop containing amongst other tools a double spindle horizontal boring machine, a double-spindle vertical boring machine, high-speed heavy cutting lathes of various sizes, large chuck lathes, slotting machines, band saws, etc. The greater part of this fitting shop is equipped with benches and vices, and here the smaller sized turbines are bladed and completed. The cranes in each of these shops are electrically driven.'

The electric power station at Palmer's, again prior to 1909. The 1920s guide to the yard, which seems to underline the yards self-sufficiency at every turn, commented: 'The company does all its own electrical work. The current for the works at Jarrow is supplied from a central power station in which it is generated from

alternators driven by internal combustion engines using the cleansed waste gases of the blast furnaces as their motive power.

The station, one of the largest of its kind in the United Kingdom, consists of seven National Gas Engine Company's vertical gas engines and one 8-cylinder National Gas engine. In addition the instillation comprises transformers, rotary converters, air compressors, etc, and an up-to-date remote control switchboard, handling high tension current at 5750 volts, and so arranged to enable the station to run in parallel with the Newcastle Electrical Supply Company's system.

For many years a local landmark, the wooden tower of the Electricity Generating Station.

The Right Hon Sir Charles McLaren, Bart MP. He joined Palmer's in 1885 and in 1897 was appointed chairman. Born 1850 in Edinburgh, educated at the city's university, he was called to the bar in 1874, enjoying a large practice as a mercantile joint stock company and railway lawyer. Other occupations included chairman of the Metropolitan Railway Company and the Tredegar Iron and Coal Company in South Wales. In 1877 he married Laura, only daughter of H.D. Pochin of Bodnant Hall, Denbighshire who was a director then deputy chairman of Palmer's for many years. Like Palmer, McLaren was a Liberal MP, representing the Bosworth Division of Leicestershire, where he owned the Croft Granite Quarry and Adamant Works and was a large employer. He owned considerable estates in Denbighshire, Carnarvon and Flintshire including the seaside resort of Prestatyn. In 1904 the newly launched staff journal, the

*Palmer Record,* presented a profile of McLaren. Reading it today it is easy to imagine it provoked very different reactions amongst the people of his day:

'One of the most interesting tendencies of the present day is that of attempting to introduce the business element into the conduct of our national affairs, illustrating the feeling which is growing in our midst, that it is on commerce that the real power of the nation rest. "The leaders of industry are the captains of the world", as the saying is, and never more so than at the commencement of the twentieth century. Those who create great industries and those who control them occupy a position in the world of influence and power which makes any knowledge of their careers of public interest. The movements of a trust magnate are chronicled with as much minuteness as those of an emperor and men weigh every phrase of the great financiers to detect his next move even more critically than Mrs Galop dissects Shakespeare's immortal lines to discover Bacon. What is this but the recognition by men that power and authority are vested in capital, which rightly administered, will make for national well being and strength and the common good.

Mr McLaren has devoted much attention to the question of British industrial supremacy, and is convinced that, so long as the British manufacturer and the British workman are prepared to adapt their methods and rules to the conditions of modern trade, there is no fear of our losing the position we now hold in the world's markets. Like so many steal and iron men in this country he has visited the principal steel making concerns in the United States and is impressed by the superiority of American methods over those in vogue here. He sees no reason why our trade should be handed over to the trusts across the Atlantic so long as we can make use of their ideas.'

The visit of the Channel Fleet Contingent to Palmer's yard. As the town depended on the yard, the yard depended on the orders such men would place and as they toured the facilities it seems almost the whole town would be involved in the welcome. In this image can be glimpsed the Mayor and in  the centre, Charles Palmer. True to its name, the *Palmer Record* recorded this visit and the subsequent speeches for the workforce's benefit:

'The Mayor, in the course of his address, said that on behalf of the inhabitants of the town he offered the men a cordial welcome. Jarrow had for many years a close connection with the Navy. It might interest the visitors to know that the yard in which they stood sixty five vessels of war had been built for the British Government. The first warship constructed there was the *Terror* in 1854, a floating battery intended for the destruction of the forts at Cronstadt during the Crimean War. This vessel was built and armour-plated within the short space of three months. Since that date the Palmer company has built many notable battleships and cruisers, and in fact, every description of fighting craft. He regretted the fleet did not include a Jarrow built vessel, but they knew that the company's productions had done, and were doing good service elsewhere. The people of Jarrow were proud of the achievements of the Navy. While they hoped that our present peaceful relations with other countries would remain undisturbed, they did not doubt that if a day of reckoning came, the 'handy men' would emulate, if not surpass, those great deeds of history which had made the British Navy feared and famous in every clime and on every sea.

Sir Charles Palmer also addressed the men and welcomed them to Jarrow Vice-Admiral Lord Charles Beresford was one of his best and oldest friends, and he (Sir Charles) was determined to be there that day to take part in the interesting proceedings, and to do honour to his men.

On the proposal of Commander A'Court hearty cheers for the Mayor, Sir Charles Palmer and Admiral Cleveland were given by the men, after which, headed by the band of the 1st DRE (Vols) they marched to the Mechanics' Institute where dinner was served.'

Locomotive number 14 one of two delivered new to the Palmer's yard in 1906. Just as the various organs of the human body can only function when linked by countless lengths of arteries and veins, a  private railway system helped keep the various sectors of Palmer's works running together as a whole. According to many reports the Jarrow works alone contained around twelve miles of running lines and sidings. If all this track was laid end to end along the Metro route it would stretch roughly from Jarrow to South Gosforth. Around fourteen shunting locomotives were employed to keep wagons moving on this system. Photographs sometimes show as many as five locos operating close to each other and it would be interesting to know how this work was co-ordinated and if collisions often occurred.

Reproduced below is an entry in the *Palmer Record* describing the specifications of the company's then newest locos, Nos 13 and 14, and the uses they would be put to.

'Nos 13 and 14 were made by the neighbouring firm of R. and W. Hawthorne, Leslie and Company limited at their Forth Banks Works, Newcastle upon Tyne, and have a handsome and powerful appearance. They are built for standard gauge, are 21 feet long overall and have five feet 6 inches wheel base, with four wheels coupled: two outside cylinders 14 inches diameter and 22 inches stroke: copper fire boxes with 9 square feet grate area; 575 square feet heating surface, giving steam at 150 lbs per square inch working pressure; steam breaks in addition to hand breaks, for convenience in handling. The new locomotives are about 25 per cent heavier and can haul loads 50 to 60 per cent heavier than the twelve locomotives formerly used in handling the same traffic. The greater power of these engines has already proved of much benefit on the heavy inclines and sharp curves of the blast furnaces and steelworks railways and has considerably expedited the work of these departments.'

Although such steam locomotives often appear quite romantic now, the smoke and smell produced by one can be considerable and the idea of twelve operating all day in the centre of Jarrow now would probably trigger calls for a public enquiry. Note also how exposed the sides and back of the cab are. Although this would have advantages in warm weather, the fire would provide little heat for the crew in winter. Finally if you are wondering where the coal was kept there would be a bunker below the windows fillable from just behind the tank and accessible from the inside of the cab. However, the fireman would have to do some judicious manoeuvring to shovel and stay out of the driver's way.

The SS *Lapland* in Palmer's graving dock Hebburn, *circa* 1920. *Below*: A general view of the Hebburn yard including the distinctive overhead cranes.

Six views of the
'sectioning' of the SS
*Cadillac* at the
Hebburn yard of
Palmer's. The
authors believe this
work took place over
April 1930 and
involved the ship
being cut in three
and the mid section
replaced. The
photographs show
the bows leaving the
old section. The
bows afloat on the
Tyne. The old section
being towed out. The
new section coming
into the dock. The
new section nearing
the engines in dock
and finally the
completed ship ready
to undock. While
such operations
saved money on
construction costs
and were welcome
work during slack
years such vessels
apparently had a
poor reputation for
safety with several
breaking apart in
heavy seas.

A 1920s guide
describes the
Hebburn shipyard
which once covered
forty acres:

'The river frontage is
1,500 feet, and has
many fitting out
jetties, dolphins and
quays. In this yard
vessels up to 700 feet
long can be built,
and there are seven
berths. A large gantry
is placed between the
two berths next to
the dock at the east

end of the yard. This gantry which is about 950 feet long and 900 feet high at the river end, is composed of massive steel columns and trusses carrying a line of rails on top. Running on the rails and spanning the two berths are two powerful 'Toplis' patent level luffing cranes with an outreach of 75 feet. The shipyard is well equipped in every respect. The main platers' shed covers a very large area, and is fitted with machinery of the most up-to-date type. To the south of this shed, and served by three lines of rails connected with the London and North-Eastern Railway, is the stacking-ground for plates and angles. This is commanded throughout all its area by a large electric travelling crane running on two pairs of rails separate from the rails for traffic. The dock is well equipped and has special facilities for the repairing of oil-carrying steamers, up-to-date arrangements being provided for water testing the oil tanks. There are three powerful hydraulic capstans for the warping of steamers in and out of the dock.'

SHIP REPAIRING
CONSTRUCTIONAL ENGINEERING
GALVANISING

**PALMERS HEBBURN COMPANY LTD**

JARROW & HEBBURN-ON-TYNE

STRUCTURAL STEELWORK · SHIP REPAIRS · GALVANISING

An advert for the yard from a post-Second World War industrial journal.

The SS *Gripsholm* entering Hebburn Palmer's in the 1920s. The *Gripsholm* was built in 1925 by Armstrong Whitworth for the Gothenburg New York Service. She was the very first diesel powered transatlantic liner and could carry 1,643 passengers in first second and third class accommodation. She became a Red Cross ship during the Second World War, was rebuilt and modernised in 1949 but kept her original diesels until she went to the breaker's yard in Italy in 1966.

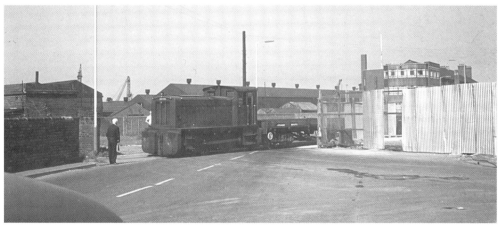

A Ruston industrial diesel locomotive leaving Hebburn Palmer's yard. Jarrow and the surrounding area was once criss-crossed with industrial railways, often forcing drivers to wait while they trundled across the road with a collection of wagons. By the early 1980s they had all pretty much gone, however the closure of the line between Monkton Cokeworks and Jarrow Staith was a mixed blessing for local people. The replacement road service involved around 200 heavy lorry journeys each day.

Workers in the Hebburn shipyards posing for informal photographs, *circa* 1956. Such 'workers' photographs often contrast quite well with much 'stiffer' official images. Included in both images is Allan Winton who went on to become one of the founder members of the Jarrow Art Club.

In the 1930s there were several campaigns to encourage the young unemployed of Jarrow to emigrate. Understandably, many were not keen on that idea. Con Shiels, however, had the much more agreeable offer from Cambridge University students to spend time in the Horesbery countryside helping local farmers. Con recalls:

'It was great to get away from Jarrow and out into the county. They even brought our dole out to us – six shillings a week. I still have photographs of us on the farm. Even though they were very kind to us we were still conscious of the difference between us and the University students (one of whom is in the back row in the black shirt). They had a confidence and a well-fed look that unfortunately our way of life in Jarrow didn't let us match.

At home all of our amusements were done without cash. Everything had to be of the invention of our own mind, what we could think of, because there was no money. I never, ever, got pocket money. In the early 1930s there was my mother and father and us six children and they were getting one pound and twelve shillings a week for all of us.

I think that outdoor activity must have been the saviour of our health because the grub we were getting was pathetic. Now when I look back on it I think how on earth did we manage. We used to go up the shop for broken biscuits because they were cheaper. Jam on bread was literally jam on bread! No butter or margarine in the middle. Bread and dripping was what we were fed on. A main meal was fish and chips out of the fish shop because that was only a penny for a fish and penny for chips. Meat was practically non existent. You might get chicken if you were taken into hospital.'

# Jarrow Gasworks

Three views of Jarrow Gasworks. The date is some time prior to 1924 and, we believe, after 1913.

A group of men working in what appears to be the gasworks' machine shop. The man middle right is believed to be Walter Hislop. While compiling this book the authors were unable to find very much information about the gas industry in Jarrow. Around 1864 the shareholders of the Jarrow Gas Company apparently voted to become part of the South Shields Gas Company. This appears to have been a take over of the Jarrow company rather than a merger. We don't know if the infrastructure was physically merged, but the Shields' company appears to have extensively rebuilt and enlarged the Jarrow plant in 1876 and again in 1913. Around 1880 the company engineer, Mr Warner, was responsible for a mechanically operated stoking device which apparently caused much interest within the gas industry. The architectural style in the three views reproduced here is similar to that at South Shields Gasworks. Around the turn of the century the company was using the works to supply Hebburn and parts of the Boldons.

Two photographs which are apparently of Jarrow Slake although the authors are unsure whether they are taken in Jarrow at all and would appreciate further information. *Above*: This is possibly one of the workers on the Slake. Behind is what appears to be the Jetty although the far end seems different to every other shot we have seen of the area. *Below*: Locomotion No 1. The caption on the back of this photograph claims this is a posed view of the loco in shop grey at the Slake and that this was a popular location to picture North Eastern Railway locomotives. This could be looking due north from Tyne Dock with the Jarrow Hall area in the background. Some of the bulky objects on the horizon being the Shell Mex tanks seen elsewhere in this book. The '1825' on the sides suggests the occasion for the Stockton and Darlington Centenary in 1925.

Monkton Cokeworks. The cokeworks was very much a local landmark. During darkness a flame was usually visible from one of its towers. For many locals returning from a long car journey this would be a welcome sign they were almost home. However, the works' smell was not so pleasant and it caused a great deal of concern to local residents.

The works' electrical driven coking car.

Two views of the cokeworks, *circa* 1955.

It was the nature of the town that many families had to live within sight and earshot of heavy industry. The Nellist family lived in Franklin Street near to Jarrow Metals. Clockwise, from top left: Elizabeth Nellist and her children Michael and Maureen with their friends Ann and John Douglas. John Nellist (nicknamed 'Pud') at his Hebburn allotment. Maureen outside their house, *circa* 1955. Maureen and Mark, *circa* 1956.

For many years Bill Connor was well known in the town as the man behind T. Fraser the decorators as well as being active in local charity work. Bill recalls:
'I left school on the Friday lunchtime at twelve o'clock and as I was going home I passed Fraser's the decorators. It was one of the town's old established firms. It was formed in 1866 by a father and his two sons. I wanted a job so I called in to see if there was any work. As I was going in, there was a lad coming out. He was called Taylor and his father carried the flag for the Salvation Army. He was packing up and going into Hawthorn Leslie's so I got his job at a penny an hour, four and tenpence a week. I had to wear a little woodwork apron and start at ten to eight, ten minutes before the men started work. I was also told that when I came to work I had to have my shoes polished. If they weren't properly polished I would have been sent home to do it and fined a

William Connor in the Services.

penny. I did my full four years as an apprentice and won several national certificates for painting and wood graining in the process. The first year I got two firsts and a second and the second year I got one first and two seconds and Mr Fraser told me I was going back! He thought standards were very important and took the competitions seriously.

Later, I was made foreman and then we were all called up into the Army. I came out of the forces with my Army suit, I got off the train at Jarrow and walked down the footbridge stairs and Fraser came out of Petries the hairdressers in Grant Street. "Connor," he says. "Are you not working." I told him I had just finished. He said, "Will you do me a good turn. Will you write a shop sign for me." I said yes and on the Monday I did the sign. I was just finishing it when he came around in his red car and said, "Will you repair the gold leaf on the Picture House staircase?" So I did that and the jobs just kept coming for ten weeks. I joined permanently and became shop foreman. I would mix the colours because ready-mixed colours were very limited then and if you wanted anything you had to mix it. I also cut the glass for shop windows. We had a big table in the shop for cutting plate glass and it used to take four of us to pick up the sheets and drop them on it and I had to walk over it to cut it.

We gradually built up the business. Often we would just start doing a fairly small job for a company such as painting signs. We did than for Lennig's, the Jarrow arm of the Rohm and Haas company. For the big wall sign that faced the river we painted 'Lennig's' in big five foot letters. Then Fraser told me if I put a hundred pounds into the company I could become a director and although it was a lot of money at the time I took him up on his offer.

Then we did the Shell Mex Works by the river. One Sunday, Billy Person and I were painting the word, 'SHELL' in eight foot letters on one of the tanks. With something that size you start from the middle and work your way out and we left the 'S' out so we could balance it up. About half past two the heavens opened and we had to leave the job. Then the police got in touch because we left the word 'HELL' in plane view! I tried to explain what we had been doing, but they didn't seem to take it in and I had to go out and put a big tarpaulin over the side of the tank until we could finish the job. I thought we were going to lose the whole job over the fuss. Then house painting began to die down and we had to expand the company into industrial painting. Around that time I became president of the Master Painters' Association. We started doing workingmen's clubs all over the North East.

Sometimes we had to have some give and take with the firms because although times were better, they weren't always good. When I was lying ill in South Shields Hospital, Emerson, who ran Shell Mex came in and said, "What's your financial situation Billy?"

I said, "I couldn't care less."

He said, "Put your accounts in and they'll be paid," and even though the work wasn't completed by that time, they were paid. On the other hand some firms would come to us and say, "We need some work doing now, but we can't afford to pay you," and we wouldn't send the bill in until they could.'

The Shell Oil Tanks, *circa* 1925.

Reyrolles Works, Hebburn.   6438

A Monarch Series postcard of Reyrolle's factory Hebburn. Wilfred Pollard recalls: 'I must be one of only one or two people left alive who had met Mr Reyrolle. I had been playing football with a few of my mates beside the factory and near the office windows. Suddenly there was a knocking on one of them and it was Mr Reyrolle. He beckoned me over and told me that we were interrupting the staff quiet hour and would we go and play somewhere else. When I was fourteen, a short while after in October 1918, I started serving my time at the factory. The First World War was still on. We all started as what was called a probationer. My apprenticeship proper began at sixteen. We would start at seven in the morning and work till five thirty. After work we would often have to be at the Marine School in South Shields for evening classes at seven o'clock. That was three nights a week for five years. I became a chargehand, in charge of a section, then a production engineer. I remember a Lieutenant Colonel came to the works as a sort of welfare officer. He was a bit of a square peg in a round hole because he was used to the army way of doing things. He couldn't get away with the idea that his orders wouldn't always be carried out and he would need to check that they had.'

Olive Goldsbrough remembers her time at the factory: 'When I went to work as a tracer at Reyrolle's, I would walk all the way to work from Monkton. It was through a cow field. I would jump a little stream and walk through a load of mud. Then when they were building Campbell Park Road there was a pathway down beside the pumphouse at the lakes. Then it would be down a bank, up the other side and through Hebburn Park. If it was a windy day the water would come over the bank and I had to dodge that as I walked. At work I would go over the men's drawings, copying them in ink on to waxed linen paper. The copies lasted longer than the original paper drawings if they were going to be used time and time again.'

Long's meat wagon, early 1940s. Included are: Jackie Brown in the striped shirt and Albert Lenney and Ralph Lenney standing. The lorry was used to deliver meat to butchers all over Jarrow from the company's premises in Wood Terrace. Some customers included: Mallen's of the High Street, Robinson's on Monkton Road, Campbell's and Tommy Reid of Ormonde Street, Joe Potts of Grange Road and Straker's of the Market Square. Sacking was often placed over the meat to allow the men to climb on to it if needed to reach a butcher's order.

Ralph Lenney in front of a Jarrow and Hebburn Co-op van, late 1950s. The garages were based at Salem Street in Jarrow.

# Jarrow Steelworks

After the closure of Palmer's and the demolition of the famous cranes the yard still contained valuable assets. The harbour had been deepened for the launch of battleships, reasonably good rail connections were in place and of course Jarrow now had a large pool of highly skilled but very under-employed workers. The terms of closure precluded shipbuilding, but it was possible one or more of the sectors of the great productive process could be revived.

In her book Ellen Wilkinson notes how in October 1934 a man with wide experience of steel making, T. Vosper Salt, came to Jarrow and noticed the site's potential for a steelworks. The riverside facilities would allow the easy importation of foreign iron ore at a time when the relative price of local supplies was rising. A report prepared for Salt by leading steel consultants Henry Brassert and Co suggested that a Jarrow steelworks was a foregone success. Wilkinson also comments that the promoters thought that while a modern steelworks of the day could produce ingots for about 78s a ton, a similar works at Jarrow could shave more than 10s a ton off that price. Yet this efficiency was to dam Salt's proposal.

In Britain steel production was inefficient; often in old or under-used plant, but the price of steel was supported by 33.3% tariffs on imported steel and by the British Iron and Steel Federation, which represented owners interests. The last thing Federation members wanted was someone like Vosper Salt, building a big new steelplant, such as he proposed, at such an ideal location as Jarrow.

The Brassert Report was submitted to the industry body in 1935 and according to Wilkinson, pressure was brought on London financiers to stop the syndicate raising capital. It seems many MPs who sniffed impending war were behind the Jarrow project, but they could not outmanoeuvre the steelowners. By 1935, British demand for steel was greater than even Brassert predicted, but according to Wilkinson, the North East steelowners argued the increase would be better met by extending existing works, rather than a new plant, justifying a policy of non co-operation to the proposers of the Jarrow works. As the Federation seemed to be effectively distributing raw materials and orders, their non co-operation would make the works a bad investment. By July 1936 Salt's works and Jarrow's hopes of a new mass employer were dead. The following October came the Jarrow March.

Eventually the steelworks proposal was revived although on a smaller scale than proposed by Salt. This view shows the inside of the Consett Works Group Steelworks, Angle Mill.

*Below*: A group of Italian operatives training at the works on handling steel strip.

# Hebburn Colliery

HEBBURN COLLIERY. (410.)

A Monarch series postcard image of Hebburn Colliery. We suspect the date is around 1910 and this is looking from an area called Smoky Row, just of Wagonway Road.

An advertising card featuring the Hebburn Colliery Prize Band. The band was formed in 1879 and disbanded following the colliery's closure in the 1930s.

# Jarrow Metal Industries

A series of photographs showing work in progress inside Jarrow Metal Industries in Western Road. The company was owned by the Armstrong Whitworth Group. The photographs were apparently taken during the Second World War and show, above, a line of 1000 lb bomb moulds being poured and, below, the removal of the bomb moulds from the pit and the bomb cases being turned out.

Jarrow Metal Industries. *Above*: Men working on a core for a turbine casing.
*Below*: Setting up a mould for a large roll casing.

*Above*: The Physical Test Room at Jarrow Metal Industries. *Below*: A core for a turbine casing.

# The Mercantile Docks

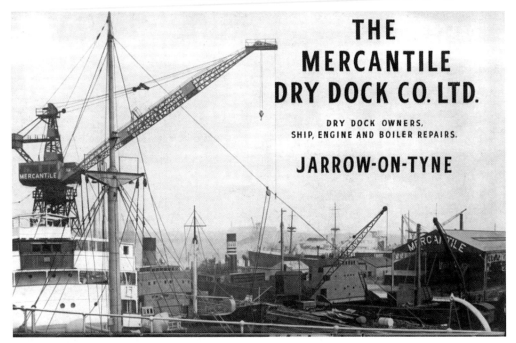

THE
MERCANTILE
DRY DOCK CO. LTD.

DRY DOCK OWNERS,
SHIP, ENGINE AND BOILER REPAIRS.

JARROW-ON-TYNE

A trade advertisement for the Mercantile Dry Dock Co. The Mercantile Dock Company can trace its line of descent back to 1885 when Mr Gavin Smith began operations as a ship repairer in the Jarrow Slake area. Realising the advantages a dry dock would bring to his business, he acquired land at Hall's Dock, Jarrow, and began construction work on what was to become the Mercantile Number One Dock. Apparently his grasp of the economics of his business was not what it might have been. In 1887 the Mercantile Dry Dock Company was formed to take over the work of completing the dock and although Gavin Smith became the first managing director of the new company he had resigned his position before the dock was completed in 1889. His

The Mercantile Dock site around 1825 then called Hall's Dock.

departure reputedly came about 'after a considerable amount of conversation and pressure.' Even before the completion of No 1 Dock, work had begun on No 2 Dock, it was finished in 1892. The company spent the remainder of the nineteenth century in fairly perilous condition. However, in 1899 two new appointments were made to the company. A Newcastle shipowner, Mr J. Tully became chairman and Mr M. James, who had worked as a navel architect, became general manager. Their arrival appears to have revitalised both the methods of production and the order book and the company went into the twentieth century both developing the works and docks and expanding their area of river frontage. By 1925 the company appears to have been in a much better financial state than the neighbouring Palmer's yard, and in the mid 1930s the Mercantile was one of the few regular employers operating in Jarrow. The demands of the Second World War on the yard's infrastructure and even before the dawn of peace, a modernisation programme was in place. By 1956 planning for a No 4 Dock at a cost of around a million pounds was well advanced.

*Right*: Demolition work in progress on the Mercantile Dock and offices.

An artist's impression of the Tyne Improvement Commission's Jarrow Staith prior to completion. An older coal staith arrangement can be seen in the top left of the picture. When complete, the staith was to feature three shipping towers with a radial travel of 95 feet. Coal being discharged from 20 or 10 ton railway trucks into three teeming hoppers (top right area of picture). The coal would then be fed on to 42 inch belt conveyors which were to stretch around a thousand feet in a journey across Blackett Street to the staith.

Construction of the coal conveyer over Blackett Street, 1935.

The collier *Hudson Strait* loading at Jarrow Staith. Opened officially by the Duchess of York on 28th July 1936, the staith was constructed to largely ship coal produced by John Bowes and Partners. The Bowes Railway was used to carry coal from the Marley Hill area to the staiths. Marley Hill Colliery was re-opened by John Bowes around 1840 under the name of the Marley Hill Coal Company. Charles Mark Palmer joined the company in 1845 and is credited with increasing coal and coke production from around 48,000 tons to 270,000 tons by 1847. Bowes described him as so knowledgeable of the coal trade and so sharp in business that he easily out manoeuvred many of the old established companies and for this alone was detested by many Newcastle merchants. Palmer thought the company was being overcharged for shipping coal via rail to Gateshead so around 1854 the company bought and extended the Springwell and Kibblesworth wagonways to Jarrow. By this time Palmer's yard had built and proved the screw driven collier the *John Bowes* a success, which revolutionised the transportation of coal to London.

*Right*: An advertisement for the John Bowes Coal Group.

A sentinel diesel locomotive on the Bowes Railway close to Oak Street. Behind is the former Armstrong Whitworth building and to the right the site of the former Jarrow Power Station.

A hired British Rail diesel shunter on the Bowes Railway during the last week of operation, close to Christmas 1985. Since the line's closure, much of the route in Jarrow has become a footpath. Part of the railway still remains operational around Springwell as the Bowes Railway.

Members of Jarrow Constabulary marching in the Mayor's Sunday Parade, 1965. It is believed those in the 'flat caps' towards the front are special constables. The reports of bawdiness and licentiousness in the local papers make interesting reading. In 1931 a sixteen-year-old youth faced Jarrow Police Court charged with having damaged an orchestral tambourine. Theatre Royal Manager, Edward Howitt, stated that about 7.10 pm, while a performance was in progress, a firework was thrown from the gallery into the orchestra and it struck the drummer's tambourine. James Henry Waggot, drummer, said that he saw the firework coming and ducked his head, but it struck him on the neck and then fell on to the tambourine and made a hole in it. PC Morrell stated that he was called to the theatre and saw the accused who said he had just thrown the cracker as a joke and did not think he was doing any harm and it was November the 5th. The Mayor imposed a fine of 10s and 10s damage.

Members of Jarrow Police taking part in a mid-Tyne better driving rally, 1959.

A trade advertisement for George Wilson Gas Meters Ltd showing the company's premises on the Bede Trading Estate. The estate was part of a post-war response to the region's employment difficulties. Work began on clearing the site for the Bede Estate in March 1946. The land had been derelict since the 1930s, having been used prior to that point by the chemical industry. It had been left in a very bad state, covered in industrial waste and the remains of buildings and criss crossed by old tunnels and drains. Clearance work was complete by the September of 1946, the first factory was occupied in May 1947.

A factory under construction on the estate. Note the houses behind.

# FAMILY ALBUMS

*Marriage … Family Groups … Children Playing … New Houses …*
*Pretty As A Picture …*

Olive Goldsbrough on the day of her wedding to
George at St Paul's Church in 1958.

Elizabeth Nellist and her five-month-old son John, *circa* 1939.

Members of the Tweddell family.

Con Shiels (right) and Vim Kelly in Salem Street, 1940.

Con Shiels and Sarah Scullion on their wedding day, 6th April 1940.

Con Shiels and Sarah Scullion's wedding party.

Members of the Shiels family.

The marriage of Navel Officer D. Whittaker to Mable Legge at St Paul's Church, Jarrow, *circa* 1941. W.G. Pearson was the best man.

William George Pearson, back row, right, with members of his family in the back garden of Harry Milburn, his half brother's house in London. Also included in the group is the then Mayoress of Jarrow Lizzie Bell. They are pictured prior to attending a Royal Garden Party at Buckingham Palace. Mr Pearson escorted his niece Miss Mary J. Bell (right of picture).

Shiels family members in their back garden at 15 Langley Terrace. Included are: Con Shiels Junior, Con Shiels Senior, Suzy Shiels and Hanna Eling.

Moya Shiels and Con Shiels Junior, Falmouth Drive, in 1959.

Con Shiels in his garden, Falmouth Drive, 1952.

John and Diana Daniels on their
wedding day.

Irene Daniels in the back garden of the
family home in Langley Terrace, 1942.

The marriage of Mr and Mrs Cyril Daniels in 1950. The group are outside of
the Station Hotel, Hebburn. Included are: Clara Smales, Maude and Dorren
McChenery, Ted Dawson and Alan Lewis.

Ted and Olive Crooks on their wedding day. Ted recalls:

'During the General Strike I experienced what it was like to have no money coming into the family. It was hard but they were not on strike for the fun of it. It was very important at the time. In the colliery areas people helped each other out if they could. If there was a wedding someone would make scones, someone else would make a cake and so on. If there was a funeral the same thing would happen. I was brought up in the Methodist way but in the Hebburn Colliery area we had all sorts of denominations like the Hebburn Free Church and the Salvation Army.

During the strike there were blacklegs of course, I think it was mainly the deputies, and it reflected badly on their children. It wasn't the children's fault but there was some bad feeling. I was going to the Colliery Board School, but I deliberately fluffed my exams for the higher school because I knew that my father could never afford to buy me the school uniforms and books I would have needed to attend.

At school I was a master's monitor along with a mate of mine. We used to go around all the classes first thing in the morning and collect the ha'pennies from any children who wanted milk. Then when the milkman came we would help distribute the bottles of milk. We would get each class attendance list for each day and at the end of the week work out the average attendance. The final figure was always worked out very carefully because there was a reward of half a day off for the school with the best attendance and of course everyone wanted that.

I finished school at fourteen and got a job as an errand boy. Then at sixteen I became an apprentice shipwright at Hawthorne Leslie's. At twenty-one I was transferred to the joinery section and became secretary of the Jarrow Branch of the Shipwrights' Society. I've been a member of the union ever since and also a member of the Labour Party. Later I became a councillor and then had to get used to people coming up to me in the street with their problems such as house repairs that weren't getting done, or they wanted to move house because they were in the wrong area and I had to approach the council officers to get something done. In 1968 I became Mayor of Jarrow.'

Members of the Daniels family including Sarah, Bob, Tom and John in Wear Street in 1916. They are very close to the site of Palmer's Hospital.

A chapel group at Jarrow, 1937.

Elizabeth Nellist, her daughter Elizabeth and twins Michael and Maureen, *circa* 1950.

Members of the Winton family outside 22 Princess Street, Jarrow in 1932. Included are: Jean, Alan, Bobby and Louise Winton.

Violet May Connor, wife of well-known local businessmen Bill, 1952.

Jenny, Sandra and Billy Tweddell, Finkle Terrace, 1960.

A portrait of Caroline Jamieson. She originated in Bermuda. In 1868 she married a Jarrow seaman and returned with him to the town. They settled in Ferry Street at No 62.

Alexander Jamieson outside his newly built house in Lindisfarne Road where he lived with his wife Agnes. Family ties were often preserved during moves to new estates. The day after they moved in, their daughter Agnes and her husband Ralph Lenney moved into the house next door.

*Left*: Jarrow Royal Navy seaman Thomas Haswell Lenney, 1940. He joined the Navy in March 1940 and took part in the battle of Calais. On the 20th February 1941 he joined HMS *Exmoor*, which had been built by Vickers Armstrong (Tyne) Parson's and was completed on 1st November 1940. He was reported missing in action on the 25th February 1941. That following July the sum of £1 16s 7d was forwarded to his mother as wages outstanding.

# SECTION FOUR

# AROUND JARROW

*Trains And Trams … The Jarrow Ferry … Ormonde Street … Local Shops For Local People … The Bede Gallery …*

Ormonde Street, *circa* 1956. The town was described in *Industrial Tyneside 1928*:

'Jarrow (pop 34,980) carries our thoughts back to the eighth century, when the Venerable Bede lived at the monastery whose church still stands just outside the town. But except for the church there is nothing venerable about the town, which is entirely modern, and cannot by any stretch of the imagination be considered attractive. It has the misfortune to be the flattest of all the Tyneside towns, lying almost entirely below the hundred-feet contour line, and with flat and rather uninteresting country behind it. Modern Jarrow sprang into existence almost entirely as the creation of Palmer's shipbuilding company which was founded in 1851, and upon this it is still mainly dependent. The only other works of any size to-day is the Mercantile Dry Dock Company. It is becoming a distributing centre for oil.'

Jarrow Station and Goods Yard, 1964. The station opened in March 1872. Previously trains ran from a station in Wylam Street through Monkton and on through Pelaw. Little definite information seems to exist on this station. Presumably Wylam Street would have been very handy for visitors to Palmer's yard and Charles Mark Palmer himself, although the service is likely to have been a little basic. In 1872 the town's station moved to the present site on a new line connecting South Shields through Jarrow and Hebburn to Pelaw. In 1874 an advert that recognised the railways' power to bring in trade appeared in the local press: 'Stewart's Wholesale Establishment being one the largest in Jarrow and on the corner of Grange and Monkton Road is on the direct road from Jarrow Railway Station and every person from Hebburn spending five shillings in groceries will have their fare paid BOTH WAYS.'

This completely free travel is perhaps not too dissimilar to the early twentieth-first century internet companies offers of completely free access to their customers. However, 1874 also saw some dissatisfaction in the town with the station's ability to cope with passenger levels of over 2,000 per day and this inspired a petition to the directors and shareholders of the North Eastern Railway Company. It was addressed from the Local Board of Health for the district of Jarrow, the rated inhabitants and manufacturers. A part of it reads: '... your petitioners are glad to learn that the directors are making efforts to alleviate the inadequate accommodation, but on enquiry and having been privileged to look at the drawings of the proposed alterations, we find such alterations will far from meet the requirements of this town. The present booking and parcel office will be altered and made into a first class waiting room, and will measure something like 12 feet by 10 feet within the walls. The present general waiting room will be divided by a partition through the centre and made into a (separate) ladies' and gentlemen's waiting room measuring something like 10 feet by 12 feet. The present ladies' waiting room will be done away with and used as a passengers entrance or general waiting room. The rooms now in use by the station master are to be converted into the general waiting room and will be two feet less both in length and width to what the present room is. The telegraph and booking offices will be built west from the new waiting room, with the living rooms for the station master above them.' The petitions then went on to describe these proposals as inadequate and suggest an entirely new station be built to the east.

By the turn of the century the station seems to have been thriving having a reasonably large goods shed and coal drops as well as serving as the 'dropping off point' for wagons running down to Palmer's yard.

Electric trains appeared on the Newcastle to South Shields service in March 1938. They were themselves replaced by diesel multiple units (DMU) in 1963. This change did not go smoothly. Previously workers flooding out of the Reyrolle's factory after the five o'clock whistle and into Hebburn station would find the 5.14 workers' special, nine coaches long, waiting to take them to Jarrow and all stations to South Shields. That train vanished along with the electric units and by 5.20 there were four hundred and fifty passengers filling the platform to capacity, with well over another hundred being held back at the top of the stairs by police and station staff. When the 5.20 arrived from Newcastle at 5.25 it was only six coaches long and already had passengers standing. Its doors swung open and with some difficulty workers from Newcastle and Gateshead made their way along the packed platform to the stairs. Immediately the last of their number stepped down from the coaches the rush to find space on the train started. The crowd hustled on board filling out the second class coaches, spilling into the first class compartment, then the guard's van. Passengers were heard to remark they were being packed in worse than cattle. Finally, the train pulled away leaving more than eighty intending passengers still at the top of the stairs behind the police barrier.

Passenger numbers dwindled, although they were revived slightly with the introduction of named trains and the 'Tynerider' branding. In late 1969, when the line became 'Paytrain', the staff moved out and the vandals moved in. The semi-derelict buildings were demolished in stages with some of the brickwork and one faded blue doorway lingering on under the footbridge until June 1981. This spot was often used by Jarrovians getting off the Newcastle train to dodge across the goods yard to the town and the Northern Bus Station. Indeed if passengers in the last car of a DMU bound for South Shields turned their heads slightly to the left they would usually see a steady stream of overalled and donkey-jacketed men with haversacks slung over their shoulders picking their way across the tracks. The goods yard itself gradually shut with the goods shed, the line to the steelworks and coal facilities all ending in the 1980s, although the last coal merchant did not leave the yard until around 1997. The line closed in 1981 to allow work on the Metro to begin, re-opening in March 1984. The first Metro train though was packed with enthusiasts who jumped off and bought 'first day' tickets at every machine on their journey to South Shields, then did the same on the opposite platform as the train returned to Newcastle.

Postmen pictured at Jarrow Station. This image is dated at 1898, sixteen years after the station opened. The gentleman third from the left, sitting in the front row, is Ralph Robson. In the original photograph it is obvious the brick and cement work is in a very good condition. The authors suspect this is the Newcastle bound platform.

Lascelle's Coal Depot, one of a number that clustered around the station. This one was apparently near Hill Street.

Closed and desolate. Around 1970 the now unstaffed station buildings await the demolition team.

Looking towards Jarrow town, track removal from the station is taking place in the foreground, *circa* 1980.

# The Jarrow Rail Crash

Standing on the Newcastle-bound platform at Bede Metro station looking across the tracks at the gently waving shrubbery it is difficult to picture the carnage that took place in 1915 in the area around the platform when three engines and their trains collided in dense fog. The area was then known as St Bede's Junction. Eighteen people died in the accident, the corpses of more than twelve passengers were charred beyond individual recognition, and sixty or more received varying degrees of injury.

Shortly after 7 am a heavy goods train of 38 trucks set off from Tyne Dock on a now abandoned line that ran to the east of what is now the Onwa factory. The gradient was 1 in 49, a banking engine was providing assistance. When the train reached the junction the banking engine left it ready to return to Tyne Dock. For some reason it did not receive the signal from the box at the junction. That day the area was shrouded in fog and it seems the driver was slack in his working practices. As the engine sat on the main line he had a green light glowing on the rear of his locomotive. It had been there since joining the goods train to save the inconvenience of changing them for the journey back to the dock. After a wait of over 15 minutes the fireman set off to the signal box, but felt the vibration of an approaching train as he ran along the ballast. Moments later a train from South Shields collided with it, knocking it on to the down line. Only moments later a third train, empty passenger stock from Hebburn on the down line to South Shields, ploughed into the pilot engine. The impact threw the engine back across the up line and both it and the engine of the passenger train tumbled down the embankment. The multiple impacts telescoped the first coach in the passenger train fracturing the gas lighting cylinders and fire swept swiftly through the coach.

Mr Will Watson of Sunderland had been travelling carriage and later told of a startling crash which shook the passengers. Although the carriage remained upright the impact jammed the doors and the workmen had to use their tools to batter them open. They escaped on to the track and found the carriage in

A Gateshead-based North Eastern Railway crane of the type occasionally employed to clear away crash wreckage.

flames. Although they tried to break open the side of the coach they were unable to immediately free any of the trapped passengers whose screams and groans were terrible to hear. As the fire spread they succeeded in freeing some of the men at the rear of the coach but by this time fire had involved the second carriage and soon afterwards part of the burning roof of the first collapsed pinning one man.

John George Kades described how he had boarded the train at Tyne Dock and found it to be full. After the impact he was still sitting in his seat. Although it was dark he could feel he was surrounded by wreckage that was fixing him down and could hear the groans of the other men in the compartment. Suddenly it filled with gas and then one end burst into flames. As the flames attacked the passengers at that end he heard them shriek in agony. He was almost overcome with the heat and flames, but suddenly found he was free of the wreckage and pulled himself outside the carriage and tumbled down the embankment.

Rescuers alerted by the terrific crash and the sudden sight of flames cutting through the fog soon began arriving. They included railway platelaying staff, medical staff, workmen from Palmer's yard, firemen from Tyne Dock Fire Station and soldiers from Simonside Barracks. The state of the passenger engine and the pilot engine greatly hampered their work. The former had been thrown completely down the embankment and had taken fire. The latter had been pitched half way down and was a mass of scalding escaping steam and boiling water. The fireman was trapped in the wreckage, pinned down by his foot and engulfed in steam. He was freed by two men, one of whom was the Jarrow correspondent of the *Shields Gazette*.

The injured were first evacuated to nearby houses then to the Ingham Infirmary in South Shields. Most of those pulled from the train before the fire survived, although the fireman of the pilot engine died a few days later in the infirmary. As the wreckage was slowly dismantled, a series of charred corpses were found and they were conveyed in sacks to the nearby train sheds. Around the area, workmen's bait tins, coins and other non-flammable items including a melted set of gold false teeth were found and by such means were many of the victims identified.

In the days after the crash the local press printed updates on the casualties and as they became able to tell their stories, interviews with the survivors. Mr Joseph Proud of 79 Wylam Street, South Shields, who was in the grocery business in Newcastle told how he was with seven other passengers in the telescoped carriage. Although suffering from severe bruises and shock he counted himself lucky in that he had been travelling with his back to the engine and was not thrown across the carriage by the first impact. When the second impact occurred he told of being flung out the carriage doorway: 'I found myself lying on the embankment. There had been eight of us in the carriage and four I am sorry to say would die. I picked myself up and the first man I met was Mr Guy. We got two men out of the carriage but the seats in the carriage were jammed together and held the other men by the legs. One poor soul was shouting, "Help me! Help me!" but he soon became enveloped in flames. We couldn't get near.'

An inquest into the accident was begun at Newcastle on Tuesday 21st December. We believe eighteen people died in the accident with around another eighteen sustaining various degrees and types of serious injury. Many of the deceased were so badly burned that direct identification was impossible even by relatives and the identities of the casualties only became apparent when men and women failed to appear at work or return home at night.

The crew of the *AB Gowan* ferry. Included are Captain Christie (centre) and Rowland Adam (right). Rowland Adam retired in 1938 and his career was featured in the local press:

With Jarrow Corporation adhering to its decision to close the vehicular ferry to Howdon at the end of the year, Mr Roland Adam, who has retired this week from the position of skipper of the ferry steamer *AB Gowan*, will be able to claim the distinction of being in the employ of the service for 54 years of its 55 years existence.

The vehicular service was started by the Corporation in 1883 and Mr Adam began as a landing boy on the Jarrow side on 4th February in the following year. He was then 11 years of age. Some five years later Mr Adam was made fireman and he soon became relief engine man. He was promoted to a skipper in 1916. Mr Adam has been responsible for conveying hundreds of thousands of passengers across the river and he has never had a serious accident. He is a typical example of the Tyneside waterman, cool, resourceful and very capable.

At the end of last year Mr Adam was warmly complimented by the Town Council for the way he handled the ferry boat during dense fog. Unable to make the Howdon landing, Mr Adam safely moored near the Mercantile Dry Docks although passengers were onboard for nearly four hours before they could be safely landed. Mr Adams who is 66 has lived in Jarrow since his childhood but was born in Middlesbrough he will continue to live in Jarrow in his retirement.

Mr Adam said: 'It is no use getting excited particularly when you have the responsibility in your hands for the safety of many people. Fogs and heavy gales were my chief worry.'

North Street Post Office. On the left is the picture house, on the right is the Co-op Drapery.

Inside North Street Post Office, 1936. Ralph Robson retiring being presented with a clock.

# The Jarrow Tramway

A group of Irish navvies pictured on a postcard dated 1906. Possibly some of these men were involved in the construction of the Jarrow tramway system. In 1901 the British Electric Traction Company were granted powers to build an electric line to serve Jarrow and connect it with South Shields. In May 1902 the *Tramway Gazette* reported: 'The necessity for extending along the banks of the Tyne has long been apparent, but it was not until December of last year that the Jarrow Light Railway Order gave the BETC the opportunity of opening up this new tract of country. With a population of 40,000 at Jarrow joined on to South Shields with its 100,000 inhabitants by a short line not much more than $2^{1}/_{2}$ miles in extent, good results may be anticipated.'

The Jarrow and District Electric Traction Company, was formed to build and operate a 'Y' shaped line. One of the 'top' ends would start outside Palmer's yard, the other near the railway crossing in Albert Road approximately where the aquarium shop is now. They would converge in the High Street and run through East Jarrow and part of South Shields to Tyne Dock gates. Although work began at the end of 1903, considerable delays were caused by disputes over road widening and whether the soon to be built tramway bridge over the River Don should also carry the public highway. When the system did open on 29th November 1906 the Albert Road line had been dropped and there were still problems with the western end of the line which took until 21st December to solve. The alleged uncouth behaviour of the labourers and problems in construction turned the system into a 'whipping boy' for the local papers and at least some of the public.

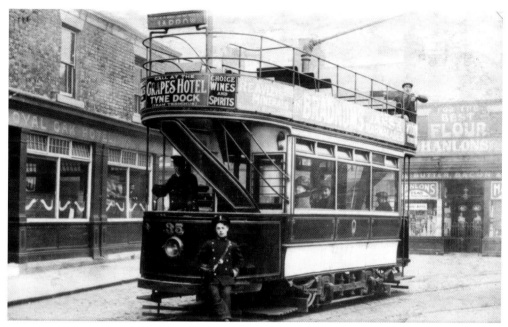

Jarrow tramcar outside the Royal Oak Hotel, *circa* 1910. This photograph seems unusually informal, the boy conductor lounging against the car and two passengers are smiling out at the camera. It also shows a car running as '35'. Only twelve cars were used by the Jarrow company, ten at any one time, although some South Shields cars did run through the town. However, this is tramcar No 35 of the Gateshead system. It was borrowed by Jarrow and not re-painted and re-numbered as No 10 for some time. The system was just over two and a half miles long with just under a mile of double track (mostly loops). Thirty-five staff were employed. Twenty-four drivers and conductors, two car washers, two labourers, two permanent way workers, two boys, one foreman, one inspector and one clerk. Eight new and two secondhand four wheel cars were obtained for the start of the service. Livery was maroon and off-white except for secondhand car No 9 which for some time was painted green. The permanent way department also had a tower car for repairing the overhead wire, which may have been a horse-drawn road vehicle rather than running on the tram rails, and a bogie wagon for track work.

In the years up until 1914 the system seems to have made reasonable returns on its £50,000 capital. However, post-war road improvements made the line vulnerable to the motor bus. On 30th June 1929 without any ceremony the last street tramcar of the twentieth century ran in Jarrow.

Northern buses at Jarrow Bus Station, *circa* 1960.

# Local Shops For Local People

The exterior of Grant and Son's shop in Ormonde Street and an advertisement extolling the shop's wares. In 1908 the Jarrow and District Electric Traction Company reached a through running agreement with South Shields Corporation and a service of electric tramcars began. These cars passed through the Shields shopping districts of Frederick Street and King Street and not unnaturally many thought this would be the death knell for Jarrow traders.

The *Jarrow Express* commented:

'Things were bad with the tradesmen before they started, but now they are infinitely worse.' The through running agreement proved to be sporadic and of course the real problems were still around two decades away. However, it may be argued that in the years when Palmer's was relatively prosperous and the town relatively isolated, Jarrow was able to build up quite a depth and variety of shops.

WATCHMAKERS to the ADMIRALTY

**GRANT & SON**

GOLDSMITHS AND
DIAMOND MERCHANTS,

63 ORMONDE STREET,

JARROW-ON-TYNE.

Have carefully re-valued the whole of their enormous stocks and reduced the prices to the : Lowest Market Quotations :

Special terms for Sports and Presentation Committees.

ALSO AT
South Shields, North Shields and Carlisle.

J.M. Amos' butcher's shop, *circa* 1900. Even at first glance it's possible to tell this is one of the better off areas of the town and the building is relatively new. The small child to the right seems to be wearing some kind of fur-trimmed robe and there is plenty of stock in the window. This shop is still standing and with the fine exterior little changed.

Members of staff of Jarrow Co-op. The location of the shop is unknown.

The Jarrow showroom of the South Shields Gas Company in Grange Road, *circa* 1920.

William Pearson at what is believed to be the opening of the Jarrow Co-op building. As far as is known to the authors, Mr Pearson was the only former Conservative MP to be president of a Co-operative Society, holding the position in Jarrow and Hebburn for twenty-five years. He said of his role: 'I'm not in the least embarrassed. My politics have nothing to do with the society job. We do not ask people when they seek membership of the Co-op whether they are Socialists or Tories. We don't have political discussions in the boardroom. We are too busy seeking business to keep up the dividend.'

Redevelopment in progress in the town centre area. The Town Hall is visible to the extreme left of the picture.

A very run down looking Ormonde Street, *circa* 1960.

The Station Hotel with construction work on the Viking Precinct underway.
Although some improvement work and rebuilding to the town centre was
needed, it is difficult to understand why such buildings were not incorporated
into the new design.

Jarrow Police Station. Note the empty ground to the left.

The Library in Bede Burn Road. It has since seen use as a community centre although it is now unoccupied.

The unveiling of the Palmer Statue outside the Palmer Memorial Hospital. The £2,000 cost of the statue was paid for by workmen of the Palmer's Shipbuilding and Iron Company Limited. However, Sir Charles is portrayed in one of his political roles, wearing his mayoral robes and chain of office, rather than simply as an industrialist.

A presentation to the Duchess of York on the day of the launch of HMS *York* from Palmer's yard. The Duke (later George VI) looks on. William Pearson is visible to the right, his niece, Mary Jane Bell is presenting the future Queen Mother with a bouquet.

A group in what is believed to be Primrose Park shortly after its official opening. Included are the Mayor, Mrs Hood and Mrs Drummond, the deputy Mayoress. In previous years the question of what was and what was not appropriate in the town's parks had occupied the attention of the town council as the *Jarrow Guardian* reported: 'The old subject of Sunday music cropped up at the council meeting on Wednesday night. Dr Weir moved an amendment to the recreation report to the effect that the paragraph dealing with bands playing in the park on Sunday should have added the words "provided no collection be taken at the gates". This was a motion which many thousands in Jarrow will agree with. As it is a very large majority of the people stay away on Sundays because there is a large white sheet spread just inside the park gates. A much better and less objectionable practice would be to sell the programmes. Ald Penman next moved another amendment which had the affect of showing how insincere are the professions of anxiety for the welfare of the toiling masses of those who make such a great ado about being anxious to study the welfare of the people. The amendment was that bands should play one Sunday in the park and the other in the Saltgrass. This was also defeated by the same majority. When the band comes down there on a week-night there are more people present than are ever seen in the park, and yet they may not have the pleasure of hearing the band on Sundays. Another important matter and one to which we think more attention should be given to, is the various items on the programme. A programme of sacred music does not mean all the latest music hall song selections from operas and so on. There are plenty of sacred tunes which can be played. The remarks of Coun Gordon that the same thing was done in churches was far fetched. Mr Gordon never went into a church yet and saw a sheet spread just inside the doors, or yet heard music hall songs or such like played. The amendment showed very clearly how much those who voted against it cared about the people. If they were so much enraptured by the quotation which Mr Hall read they had a very strange way of showing it when they would vote for the very thing which would keep the people east of Monkton Road and Monkton Terrace away from the park, their desire to elevate and benefit them being all a sham. The park was not provided simply for them to promenade and air themselves in. So long as the sheets are put down so long will the people of the areas named be excluded from the special prerogative of the few.'

The Queen's Head Hotel. Like any industrial town where hard work created a demand for alcohol, Jarrow of the 1930s saw many preaching the virtues of temperance. The Jarrow Branch of the British Woman's Temperance Association often held exhibitions in the town including one in the Lloyds Bank building that lasted for a week. It featured models which illustrated the effect of alcohol on child life, home life and industry and one poster stated that Jarrow's drink bill for a year was £235,600 which represented over £33 per family or £6 per person. The sum it was said provided work for only 132 people in the licensing trade whereas it would otherwise provide work for 1,000 people.

The altar at Drewett Park, near St Paul's Church, for the St Bede's celebrations of 1935.

Bob Bowman, front centre, with staff from Reyrolle's works who he took for a day out in Edinburgh when he retired in 1963.

The Robin Hood Public House. The road in front is the old road towards Newcastle. Before the construction of the more recent estates the upstairs windows apparently had an almost clear view of Boldon Colliery. The side of the bridge visible here is now buried beneath the new road which connected up with York Avenue. York Avenue was reputedly the first duel carriageway in the UK and at that time traffic was so infrequent many residents recall being able to use it for roller skating.

The white miners' cottages situated at the top end of the High Street near the junction of Short Row. The date is likely to be early 1930s.

Ice floating on the river Tyne alongside what is possibly Hebburn Palmer's yard. The photograph is dated 6th March 1963.

A horse-drawn van belonging to Windham Brothers Removal Contractors.

A horse-drawn ambulance. Olive Goldsbrough recalls going to hospital in a horse-drawn ambulance during the Second World War: 'Clip clop, clip clop we went, up past the cokeworks because that was the most direct route. It was either go right the way round through Jarrow, up to Hebburn, or that way and go along the Spuggy's Bridge. Later on the same horse pulled the cart for the road sweeper. I was in the hospital for two months and it was blamed on our air raid shelter. My mam used to have a coke fire going in there and I think the fumes caught my chest. Sometimes you could be in there for quite a long time.'

BEDE BURN ROAD, JARROW.

*Above*: Bede Burn Road. During the Second World War a sub-fire station, complete with emergency water tank, was built on the ground to the right.
*Below*: Park Road. The building towards the middle is now the Labour Club

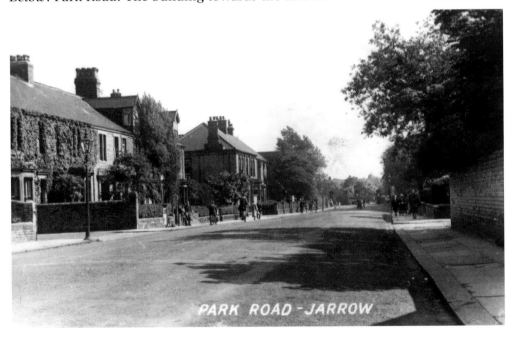

PARK ROAD - JARROW

South View Road. The building nearest the camera is now in use as the Regional Labour Party headquarters. The Labour Club is now located behind the photographer.

The Park Gates at Canning Street, Hebburn. Both this and the image above are from the popular Monarch Series of postcards.

# The Bede Gallery

Michel Foot unveiling the Jarrow March sculpture by Vince Rea, 1986. The sculpture is now on the platform at Jarrow Metro Station. Vince Rea is on the left. Michel Foot said that he preferred the building as an art gallery rather than its previous use as a nuclear bomb shelter. Vince Rea's wife, Willa, was a co-director of the gallery: 'When Vince first had the idea behind the Bede and we mentioned the idea to people everyone said, "An art gallery in Jarrow!" They thought we were mad. At that time there were very few venues for contemporary arts in the area. When Vince acquired the building it was just a derelict empty shell that had been last used by the civil defence authority twenty years ago. The inside was divided up into cubicles and full of water.

When we opened I think we were the very first venue to bring art into the working class area and do local history documentaries like Jobling and Palmer's shipyards. The gallery was very community orientated, there were never any barriers or elitism there. In the early days we used to do poetry readings. One of them was an arts snob and he got into an argument about poetry and someone punched him in the face. He had to be helped up of the floor.

In 1976 a group of students spent the summer in the gallery doing installations called "This England's Birthplace". They made a whole series of sculptures, all the way back in time to Saint Bede, with wire and thousands of old Gazettes. We also had the inflatable village right across the park and lots of performance art that involved the community. We built two thirty-five foot cranes on the roof for the Palmer's exhibition. They were erected over the weekend and then the planners came flying down saying we didn't have permission for them, but we said we didn't need it because it was sculpture, and we didn't need permission to put them on the roof. In the end they were up there for three months in all kinds of gales. They were marvellous pieces of engineering.'

Willa Rea in front of a Hoyland painting in 1990. 'We also had a reputation in the art world for bringing in international exhibitions. We had all the arts ministers coming in from the House of Commons and the House of Lords to say how wonderful the place was. Not that many of them ever did anything for us of course. We also had Edward Heath, Neil Kinnock and Michael Caine.

Every artist and every exhibition is different. Some were very precious about other people handling their work, others just left you to it. One day the television people came to do a spot on the jewellery exhibition we were having. We had tarantulas and snakes in to help with the publicity, and while we had the lids off the cases to film them, there was a power cut. Everything went black – there being no windows in the gallery – and the snakes and tarantulas were on the loose. Vince was the only one who would handle them, *The Times* published a photograph with one on Vince's hand.

It was a very interesting life and I wouldn't have done anything else in the world. We built up quite a regular clientele and I think some people got on so well the gallery was even responsible for a few marriages.'

Van Gogh exhibition at the Bede Gallery in 1974. Vince Rea with his niece, Sandra, and the Bede Gallery dog, Sullivan, are in front of Dave Pearson's interpretation of Van Gogh's potato eaters.

PHOTOGRAPHED BY
J. CONNACHER
6A, GRANT STREET,
JARROW

Jarrow Police on duty outside the Town Hall at what appears to be a royal occasion. This photograph is dated 1954.

The Queen on the steps of the Town Hall. Also included are Mayor Emily Coates and Mayoress Mrs Watson.

# CLUBS AND SOCIETIES

*Congo Cycling ... On The Stage ... Brigades And Companies ...*
*Jarrow Bowling Club ... Football Teams ... Jarrow Art Club ...*

Jarrow Masons at the Masonic hall during the twenty-fifth anniversary of Jarrow Grange.

The Congo Cycling Club on Bede Burn Road, 1902. The building behind the cyclists is the old police hostel.

While at first sight this may look like an old fire engine it is in fact a mock-up by the members of the Congo Cycling Club presumably for one of the town's many carnivals.

Backstage at Jarrow Community Centre, *circa* 1950. George Goldsbrough is on the left and in the centre is Jimmy Blair.

George Goldsbrough on stage with others at Jarrow Community Centre.

Members of Jarrow Boys' Brigade, *circa* 1930.

Jarrow members of the Durham Light Infantry, 1918. The location is likely to be Seaham Harbour.

Jarrow Bowling Club Members, *circa* 1915. The occasion is their winning of the Marshall Cup. Included are: J. Thomas, A. Mason, R. Webster, G. Clarkson, A. Judge, J. McIntosh, C. Maughan, R. Robson, P. Judge, W. Moore, A. Overton, T. Daniels and T. Lusk.

Club members, 1946. On display are believed to be the Cowan Cup, the Oubridge Cup, the Durham Singles and the Hannington Trophy.

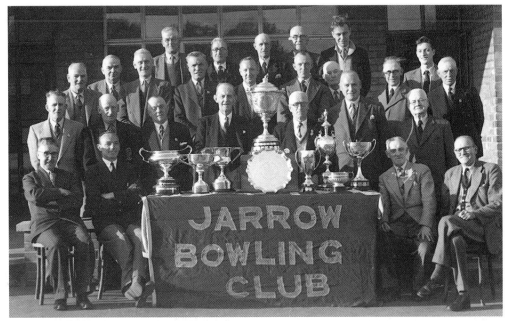

Jarrow Bowling Club members for the 1956 season.

Club members in their Jubilee year of 1965.

A boys football team at Jarrow Higher Grade School, 1913.

Members of Jarrow Ellison Villa football team 1922-23. Back row: W. Smith, W. Pigot, G. Shanky, W. Orr, W. Denning. Middle row: W. McPadden, W. Stead, J. McPadden, M. Bently. Front row: G. Carnagie, F. McMullen, A. Stead, G. Patterson, P. Bradley.

Self-taught artist Allan Winton and his family. While working in London Docks in 1949 Allan fell forty feet and broke both legs. To while away the nine months he spent in hospital he took up drawing and painting. In 1962 he became an early member of the Jarrow Art Club. He was also a member of the Federation of Northern Artists Societies.

The Jarrow Art Club was formed at a meeting on 28th February 1962 at Jarrow Community Centre in Ellison Street. Previously, in an article in the *Shields Gazette*, artist George Patterson had suggested that people in the town who had an interest in art should get together. Tom Lydon became the chairman, George Patterson, secretary, Ken Stewart, treasurer. Alan Winton joined on 10th October 1962. The Art Club, later known as the Art Group, did much to encourage art in the area. Members developed individually in style and techniques, having many works accepted in competitive gallery exhibitions, with much discussion on ideas and originality. Regrettably it disbanded in September 1996. *Top*: George Patterson, Ken Stewart, Vince Rea and Jim Lishman at an exhibition in Elders Cottage, Hebburn 1966. *Middle*: George Patterson with two of his paintings, 'Crusade' and 'Red Wine Shop'. *Bottom*: An exhibition in Christ Church Hall. Included are: the Rev Johnson, Mayor and Mayoress H. Duggan and George Patterson.

Members of Jarrow Conservative Club in Bede Burn Road prior to an official outing.

The town's MP Ellen Wilkinson (second from left, front row) at a Jarrow Girls' Training Corps, 259, presentation during the Second World War. Company Commander Dorothy Hall is also present.

# POLITICS

*Palmer For Jarrow! … The Town Hall … The Council And*
*Councillors … Public Opinion … William George Pearson …*
*Mayoral Visits …*

The 1907 Jarrow By-election result is announced outside the Town Hall. The
poll had been triggered by the death of Charles Mark Palmer, the town's
Member of Parliament. This time the victor was Labour member Pete Curran,
who had previously challenged Palmer for the seat in 1906. Here Curran and
one of his opponents, possibly Liberal Spencer Leigh Hughes, stand on a table
as the result is announced. The man in the middle is presumably the returning
officer while the bowler-hatted men may be reporters from the rival *Jarrow
Guardian* and *Jarrow Express.* Curran's victory gave the Labour Party its first
Jarrow MP. However, the name of Palmer was victorious again when Palmer's
former party, the Liberals, found another candidate who bore the Palmer name.

Sculptor Albert Toft working on 'Sir Charles' *circa* 1903. Toft was also responsible for the statue of Queen Victoria which stands outside of South Shields Town Hall. He was described as, 'a gentleman from the South who was every inch an artist.'

The death of Sir Charles at his London residence at 37 Curzone Street at one o'clock in the morning of Tuesday, 4th June 1906, could be said to mark the beginning of a new political age for the town. Jarrow was incorporated as a borough on 4th June 1875, and Palmer was one of the first on the town council, being elected 10th August that same year as representative of the Jarrow South Ward. He became the town's first mayor, although he gave up the office the following November. A seat in Parliament came when he won North Durham for the Liberals in 1874. Then in 1885 he successfully stood for Jarrow, holding the seat until his death. Apparently his last public appearance in Jarrow was in 1905 when, from the balcony of the Town Hall, he thanked the electors for re-electing him to Parliament.

The scenes at the 1874 election were described in the *Jarrow Guardian*:

The excitement at Jarrow was very great, and we regret to add that it culminated in a riot. During the greater part of the day the excitement was of a peaceful, character, and this doubtless was owing in a great measure to the arrangements of Supt Thomas Salter who, with a force of between forty and fifty men (his own staff being amalgamated by men from South Shields, Northumberland and other parts of Durham County), kept the large crowd of workmen assembled at the various booths in order. There were three booths fitted up, two in the Mechanics' Institute, Ellison Street, and one in Dr Jackson's Lecture Hall, Monkton Road. The popular colour blue and white appeared to be in the ascendant, and men, women and children vied with each other in cheering the voters brought to the poll by Messrs Bell and Palmer's agents. This could not, however, be said of the electors in favour of the Tory candidates, for it took the worthy superintendent with the assistance of his men all their time in seeing that they were allowed free progress into the polling booth. As might be expected, work at Messrs Palmer's and other large firms on the Tyne was suspended during the course of the day, and the men in large numbers assembled at the various street corners discussing the probable result of the election. Several of their fellows, more active than the rest, made a huge 'Guy' of the principal Conservative candidate, and paraded it about the streets of the town to the no small amusement of the spectators. It was stated on good authority that nearly the whole of the electors liable to vote had exercised their privilege by one o'clock. Throughout the whole of the day bands of young men and boys paraded the streets of Jarrow, but nothing occurred of a serious nature until after five o'clock in the afternoon. At that time a mob gathered outside the Mechanics' Institute and amused themselves in a boisterous fashion. A large posse of police, under Superintendent Salter, were ranged on the other side of the street, when the behaviour became very rough, and stones were flying at the police, the latter charged the mob with their batons, and a few men, women and boys were seriously injured. For an hour or two afterwards there were disturbances in various parts of the town. Stones were flying from the populace on one side, and on the other the police dispersed the gatherings in every street by freely using their truncheons. Superintendent Salter received a servere blow on the head and a number of the officers were more or less bruised. We regret very much that innocent persons have suffered in this unfortunate encounter while the guilty parties have got off scot-free. Great indignation, we think it fair to say, has been expressed by a very large number of very respectable eye witnesses at the manner in which the police used their batons when they charged the mob. Numbers of inoffensive persons, including children of tender years, have been seriously bruised, and we fear antipathy has been aroused towards the officers of the law among peace loving citizens that it will take some time to allay. A number of gentlemen have formed themselves into a committee to collect evidence and take legal advice on the conduct of the police. We take this opportunity of letting the committee know we have it on good authority that Mr Salter did not sanction the violent measures resorted to by the men under his charge, in fact we are told that he discondoned it, and did his utmost, aided by others of his sergeants, to stop it. He kept in the streets to prevent any violence on the part of his men till a medical gentleman demanded that he should go home.

The local press were hardly unbiased in elections, supporting Palmer with editorials and articles that now seems almost maniacal in their intensity.

'Palmer for Jarrow.' This is a splendid motto! Without him what would Jarrow be today? No doubt someone else might have come and started a shipyard but would the head of that business have made the name known to all the civilised world? The firm of Palmer's has been a beacon light from its first inception. They had not been long started before the energetic brain of Charles Mark Palmer solved what until then was a knotty problem – to get plates for a fighting ships' armour that would not splinter and break when struck by a shot. To him belongs the honour of inventing the rolled plate which could resist the heaviest of metal discharged at it. Another important item was the introduction of steam colliers. Here again the master brain of Charles Mark Palmer achieved highest honours in that it made work for thousands upon thousands of men today. Had the steam collier not been invented there would not be the amount of trade that exists at present on Tyneside. That one thing alone meant work for the miner, the shipbuilder, the labourer who discharges the vessel, not to mention those who put the coals into the ships. While thus laying the foundations which were to provide work for hundreds of thousands, he looked upon their physical needs. Like other places, accidents were often happening and the injured ones had to be conveyed to Newcastle. Mr Palmer built the Memorial Hospital in Clayton Street so that any workman injured while at work could be attended to at home without having to endure the torture which could not be helped while being conveyed to Newcastle. Again our railway facilities were of a very primitive kind, but he interested himself on the matter and got this remedied. There are scores of other things that Mr Palmer did that people today know very little about. Those living at the time appreciated his good works and presented him with an illuminated address in the Drill Hall in token of their appreciation for what he had done not only for the town but for their comfort and well being. Not one man then who was getting his living in the yard dreamed of such a thing as opposing Mr Palmer. Notwithstanding the fact that over thirty years have passed away since then the old love and enthusiasm burn as brightly as ever and the battle cry to-day as of yore 'Palmer for Jarrow!'

The opening of Jarrow New Town Hall by Sir Charles Palmer. The foundation stone had been laid on 9th October 1902. In addition to the Mayor and the Mayoress those present included: Lord Northbourne, the Hon Robert James, Lady Evelyn James, Mr A.M. Palmer, the Mayors of Newcastle, Durham and South Shields. A newspaper of the day gave its readers an insight into the new building: 'It has been erected in a free treatment of the classic renaissance style and the external work being carried out in red terra cotta and red brickwork. A building erected with such materials is an innovation in Jarrow, and their use has been thoroughly justified, for although it has been nearly two years in construction, every part of it looks quite fresh and new in spite of the severe test of the atmosphere of Jarrow.

The principle entrance is in Grange Road, after passing through an oak panelled vestibule in which the foundation stone of the building is exposed, the main hall and staircase is reached. The staircase is of marble with oak panelling and pilasters, and the arcading on the ground and first floors gives a very pleasing effect. The council chamber and committee rooms are on the first floor front, and adjacent are the Mayor's parlour and the Councillors' cloak room. In the council chamber the seats have been arranged in a horseshoe form with the Mayors dais at the end, and the officials table in the middle. The fittings of the chamber are in fumed oak and red morocco.

At the opposite end to the Mayor's dais is a gallery for the public. The county court is situated on the first floor, and is reached by a separate entrance and staircase from Wylam Street. The accommodation for the public is most adequate. Waiting rooms for the public and ladies are provided. The municipal officials are all housed on the ground floor in lofty well lighted offices. Adequate sanitary convenience is provided in connection with every department. The building is heated throughout by low pressure hot water, but fireplaces are provided in all rooms. The offices are all connected by a system of telephones so complete it is possible to speak from any room to any other.

The total cost of the whole building and furnishing is about £12,000. It was originally thought that about £10,000 would cover the cost but those who had given a second thought to the matter knew this was not possible. However, now the buildings are complete the ratepayers have the satisfaction of knowing that they have a substantial equivalent for the money they will have to pay.'

The Mayor and Corporation in the new council chamber. This is possibly their first meeting in the chamber. The candidates for the first election to the Town council were: EAST WARD – Thomas Brady, agent; William Henry Dickinson, butcher and farmer; Hugh McGrorty, innkeeper and builder; John Pringle, provision merchant. JARROW WARD – William Titus Baker, hotel keeper; Michel McWilliams Bradley, surgeon; Joseph Thompson Dickinson, butcher; Oliver Haynes Duffell, draper; Edward Foster, publican; Peter Edward Fox, chemist; Thomas Grey, farmer; Zeohaniah Harris, builder; John Sedgwick Lambert, boot merchant; Matthew Nixon, chemical manufacturer; Charles Mark Palmer, colliery owner; John Thomas Oswald Penman, butcher; John Slevin, grocer; Andrew Smith, house agent. WEST WARD – Charles Barritt Barnes, accountant; Philip Aughustus Berkley, engineer; George Hornsby Dexter, builder; Thomas Edwards, forge manager; Thomas Gibb, chemicalworks manager; Thomas Grey, farmer; Robert Chapman Hall, draper; William Hedly, furniture dealer; George Johnson, draper; Thomas Medd, pawnbroker; James Ridley, grocer; Hugh Shields, builder; James Wardle, innkeeper. SOUTH WARD – John Henry Dale, banker; Thomas Grey, farmer; Robert Elliot Huntley, surgeon.

A cartoon from the *Jarrow Express* of 1901. The *Express*, conservative in outlook, campaigned fiercely against free trade, arguing tariffs on foreign imports would protect British jobs. There also appears to have been several heated debates in the town on the subject. As is the case with many

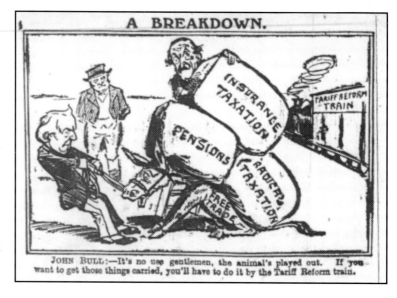

A BREAKDOWN.

JOHN BULL:—It's no use gentlemen, the animal's played out. If you want to get those things carried, you'll have to do it by the Tariff Reform train.

local newspapers, the town council often came in for some withering criticism. The following *Express* editorial entitled 'Corporation Bungling' dates from November 1901:

'For some years past our Corporation have held the unenviable character of being notorious bunglers of everything they take in hand There has not been one single instance during the last two decades to which anyone can point that has not been mismanaged from first to last. Our lighting is bad and our streets are worse. The latest piece of folly perpetrated by them has been in connection with their electric lighting and tramways scheme. Twelve months gone June they led the public to believe that everything was in apple pie order for the laying in of the electric mains. Since then, however, they have had another of those spasmodic outbreaks of which they are afflicted, and an attempt was made to change the rout of the tramways. Failing in that, the matter was allowed to lapse into abeyance, and nothing further was heard about electric lighting or anything else. Months passed over, and when the summer had given place to autumn they suddenly awoke to the fact that nothing had been done towards making a start in the shape of laying the cables for the lighting. Considering that they had the benefit of seeing and hearing what the condition of things in neighbouring towns were like where the electric light was being introduced, sensible people asked themselves what was the Corporation doing that they were so dilatory as to allow all the finer weather to go by without a start being made.

Now we have the result of their folly. A commitment was made a fortnight ago – just before the great storm – the pavement being displaced along Grange Road and a start was made to take it up in Ormonde Street this week. The flags were taken up and the soil thrown out in a heap in the gutter. The disagreeable effects of this were felt by every shopkeeper in the street. It is impossible to go to one single establishment without finding the floor within in as bad a state as the thoroughfare outside. Traffic in the street was seriously impeded by reason of obstruction caused by the flags being picked up and tool chests and other things required for the work being placed in the gutter further along. Added to all this, the tank in which the pitch is heated gave off a most offensive and nauseating effluvia. The scene of operations has now been transferred to Western Road and what state was Ormonde Street left in? Certainly far from the condition in which it was found. Where the footpath is paved the flags are replaced anyhow: here and there are gaps with no flags at all simply because they have not been put back right: and above all they are not level. It is time the town council learned if a thing is worth doing its worth doing well. They have done many foolish things, but the present performance may safely be classed as outstripping them all.'

*Right* and *below*: Requesting the pleasure of your vote. Cards produced to woo the voters in parliamentary and municipal elections.

### JARROW DIVISION.

Parliamentary Election, 1910.

Your vote and interest are earnestly solicited by

Cleadon Park,
Near Sunderland.

Printed and Published by R. Ward & Sons, High Bridge, Newcastle.

## JARROW MUNICIPAL ELECTION
### NOVEMBER 1st, 1911.

## To the Electors of the South Ward.

Dear Sir or Madam,

Four years ago, after a contested Election, you did me the honour, to elect me by a very decisive majority as your representative on the Town Council.

I have conscientously endeavoured to do my very best, not only for the interests of the South Ward in particular, but for the Town in general, and I have given my support to all reasonable progressive proposals for the benefit of the Town and its inhabitants. I have also for three years performed the onerous duties of Mayor, which were rendered more than ordinarily burdensome through the distress arising out of the severe industrial depression which unhappily existed during the greater part of this period.

I am prepared to accept nomination for re-election on November 1st, and, therefore, solicit a continuance of your support, and with the fullest confidence in your sense of fairness and justness I leave my claims for a renewal of your confidence entirely in your hands.

Yours faithfully,

M. C. JAMES

Printed and Published at the "Guardian" Office, Walter Street, Jarrow.

Some of that control may have been exercised by a number of Palmer's employees who served as councillors making the Town Hall, as has been suggested, just another part of Palmer's Works. It would be grossly unfair to claim that Palmer's men who served on the council were there simply to fulfil the wishes of the company. We are sure they served their constituents well. We happened across profiles of two such men in the 1907 volume of the *Palmer Record* which are reproduced here, although this is not to suggest they were typical of 'Palmer's Councillors.'

'Councillor Alfred Pilditch, who was elected to represent the Grange Ward in the Jarrow Town Council in April last, is one of the best known officials of the Palmer's Company. He entered the firm's service nearly forty years ago and has occupied some responsible posts, his present being that of assistant secretary. There is we can

Councillor Alfred Pilditch.

safely say, no man on the staff who has a more intimate knowledge of the past history of the concern, nor one who has been more zealous or conscientious in the performance of his duties. He has witnessed the works expand in various directions with the growing requirements of the times, and has lived through many changes of policy and management. His friends are glad to note that through it all he has managed to retain much of the buoyancy of youth, and that of late he has begun to take an active part in public and municipal affairs in Jarrow. The contest in April last was Mr Pilditch's first attempt to enter the Council, and his success was gratifying to his various friends. The voting was as follows: A. Pilditch, 419; T.T. Harvey, 328; T. Gibb, 122; majority over Harvey, 91. If attention to duty will make a good councillor, we feel sure that the electors of the Grange Ward will have no reason to regret their choice. Mr Pilditch, who is married, and lives at Grange Villa, Jarrow, has one daughter and two sons, one of whom is a Lloyds' engineer surveyor.

Councillor John Wright (*right*) was also featured in the *Palmer Record*:

'Mr John H. Wright who was on 25th June 1907 elected to fill the vacancy in the West Ward of the Jarrow Town Council occasioned by the elevation of Councillor Archbold to Aldermanic rank, consequent on the death of Alderman Sir Charles Mark Palmer, is one of the oldest officials of Palmer's Company. He entered the service of the company about forty years ago as office boy and has risen to occupy the important and responsible position of chief cashier.

Councillor Wright is best known on Tyneside through his connection with the 1st Durham Royal Engineers (Vols) which he entered as a sapper, rising through the various grades of the service to the rank of Colonel, a position which he at present occupies with every credit and distinction. We have pleasure in reproducing a photograph of the new Councillor in his regimentals, and join with his numerous friends in heartily congratulating him upon the latest honour shown him by his fellow townsmen. As in the case of Councillor Pilditch, this was Colonel Wright's first attempt to enter the council, and he was elected over his opponent by a majority of 199 votes, the poll being: J.H. Wright, 414; T. Gibb, 215.'

Reports in the *Jarrow Express* and *Jarrow Guardian* show some of the matters of that era discussed by the council members: 'Included was a petition from the hairdressers in favour of their closing day under the Order being changed from Thursday to Wednesday. The Sanitary Committee reported that eight samples of milk, six samples of whisky, and six samples of butter have been submitted to the public analyst who reports all the samples of butter genuine, three samples of milk genuine and three samples slightly below the standard, five samples of whisky genuine and one sample slightly below the standard, and the Committee recommended that letters of warning be sent out to the vendors in the cases where the samples were defective. The Committee have considered communication with the North East Joint Smallpox Hospital Board as to the temporary provision of a Smallpox Hospital and the Committee recommend that the matter be left to the Hospital Committee to deal with. The Town Clerk was also directed to call the attention of the contractor to the damage done to the box closet doors and also the overloading of the night spoil carts, and ask him to take steps to remedy these two matters.'

William George Pearson, Mayor of Jarrow in 1927, 1928 and 1929 and the town's Member of Parliament from 1931. Elected as a councillor in 1920, he represented the South Ward and also saw long service as a representative on the North Eastern Area Guardians' Committee. His name also crops up in journals and papers in association with all kinds of social and charitable work. William Pearson was a keen churchman and was a regular attendee at Christ Church. He was an active member of the Conservative Party and lived in Albert Road for a number of years.

Sometimes described as 'a bit of a one off', Mr Pearson's election to Parliament in 1931 as one of 471 Conservative MPs in the curious coalition of the National Government which followed the collapse of the previous Labour administration. Within the context of Palmer's closure the National Government is often seen as a villain, blind to much

William Pearson at a special event just after his election in 1931.

of the economic stagnation and the accompanying misery it was causing, particularly across the industrial heartlands. However, political theorists often see it in a different context, as the glue that held British democracy together at a time when extremes, particularly Oswald Mosley and the British Union of Fascists, were gaining ground. A point often made is that many of the Conservative candidates in what had been Labour seats had been chosen because they were either leftward leaning or concerned with the day's social problems. Their arrival in Parliament actually helped neutralise the more right wing elements in the party who may have been more sympathetic to Hitler.

When William Pearson was elected the economic position of the town was deteriorating. Only one ship was built at Palmer's yard and unemployment in the town had reached 6,700 – double the previous year's total. A local newspaper covered his election claiming he was winning support from both Liberals and Socialists: 'A bold bid to win Jarrow, after many years of Liberal and Labour representation in Parliament is being made by the Conservatives with their National candidate Mr W.G. Pearson and victory is confidently predicted. Mr Pearson has the support of the Liberals and also many Socialists who believe in Mr MacDonald's policy and if everyone votes there is little doubt that the National candidate will top the poll. A Jarrow invalid in London has applied to be taken to Jarrow in order to vote for Mr Pearson.'

He is pictured here in 1938 when he was invested with the CBE at Buckingham Palace for political and public services in Jarrow.

Pearson polled 21,263 votes against his Labour opponent Mr Rogers' 18,071. In the previous General Election Labour had won the seat – 22,751 to the Conservatives 13,638. While part of his success was likely due to the absence of a Liberal candidate, the fact that he was both a local and someone who seems to have placed social welfare high on his own agenda undoubtedly helped.

Declaring the election results at the Town Hall. John Daniels is on the left wearing the rosette.

A presentation at the Town Hall. Included are: Mayor Frank Dixon, John Daniels and Mr and Mrs Cromer.

Councillor Ted Crooks serving as Mayor of Jarrow on a visit to Epinay, Paris, in 1968. As part of the visit he took part in a naming ceremony for 'Avenue de Jarrow'.

Jarrow Goods Yard, *circa* 1981.

## Acknowledgements

This book was put together with the active participation of Bill Connor, Margaret Connacher, Miss O'Connor, Ted Crooks, Cyril Daniels, Colin Davidson, George Goldsbrough, Howard Goldsbrough, Olive Goldsbrough, Dorothy Hall, Peter Hedly, John Hill, Norman Holland, Derrick Knott, Justine Lenney, Michael Nellist, George Patterson, Hilda Pattie, Wilfred Pollard, Vince Rea, Willa Rea, Margaret Pickering, Jim Sayers, Con Shiels, Neil Tweddell, Sheila Tweddell, Stan Tweddell, Robert Wray, Allan Winton and members of the Winton family.

We would also like to thank Keith Bardwell, Dorris Johnson the staff of the Tyne and Wear Archives whose names, apart from Nicola's we don't have and Alison Gibson and Alastair Greeson from the Bowes Railway whose names we have just found again.

Special mention at this point for Sarah Jane April Roddam. Thanks also to the drivers on the X34. (The Stagecoach Busways one)

Photographs also provided by Ian S. Carr and George Nairn. Addition help and research Robert Wray and Dennis Boad. Proof reading Stan Tweddell. Thanks to everyone involved in the production, editing, re-editing and extensive re-editing of this book.

Additional photographs supplied by:

The Alan Havery Collection
The Bowes Railway
Tyne and Wear Archive Service
Beamish Open Air Museum
The Shields Gazette
Newcastle City Libraries,
Vince Rea/Bede Gallery

Sometimes when researching this book the trail has suddenly gone cold and captions are not as complete as we would like. Our apologies, but we still thought the photographs worth including anyway. If you have any information or photographs that might be useful in a future addition of this book lease contact the authors via the publishers.